Wakefield Press

Samela Harris was born in Adelaide. She worked as a journalist in London and Edinburgh, pausing to marry, bear two sons and spend five years as an organic market gardener in lush Surrey, England. It was there that her interest in hearty home cookery developed.

Returning to Australia as a supporting mother, Samela made bountiful shoestring budget meals the core of a secure environment for her sons. It was such an inviting world that increasing numbers of boys kept hanging around for meals – and then just staying.

Thus the House of the Raising Sons was born, and Samela's amusing tales of life with the lads and her economical recipes became a popular newspaper column. She works at the Adelaide *Advertiser* as a features writer, critic and Internet writer.

Samela is the daughter of Australian poet and social commentator, the late Max Harris.

dedicated to Max

On a Shoestring

Recipes from the House of

the Raising Sons

Samela Harris

....

Illustrated by

Brenda Maxwell

Wakefield
Press

Wakefield Press
1 The Parade West
Kent Town
South Australia 5067
www.wakefieldpress.com.au

First published 1996; revised edition 2009

Illustrations by Brenda Maxwell, Adelaide
Cover designed by Liz Nicholson, designBITE
Book designed by Kerry Argent, Adelaide
Typeset by Clinton Ellicott, Wakefield Press
Printed and bound by Hyde Park Press, Adelaide

National Library of Australia
Cataloguing-in-publication entry

Author: Harris, Samela

Title: On a shoestring: recipes from the
                 house of the raising sons/
                 Samela Harris; illustrator, Brenda Maxwell
Edition: Rev. ed.
ISBN: 978 1 86254 856 5 (pbk.)
Notes: Includes index
Subjects: Low budget cookery
                 Quick and easy cookery
Other Authors/
Contributors: Maxwell, Brenda
Dewey Number: 641.55

Government
of South Australia

Arts SA

Contents

Introduction

···

Celebrity chefs, competition chefs, reality chefs, heavyweight chefs, icon chefs, iron chefs, superstar chefs …

Cuisine has become media chic. It has become a spectator sport. The resulting food from stainless-steel industrial kitchens is bedazzlingly complex. Good grief, they make ice-cream with liquid nitrogen and creme brulee with blowtorches. No common old wooden spoon for the modern chef. They have knives, though, and seeing them screaming profanities at each other, one rather wishes they didn't. Cheftertainment is all very highly strung. And then they feed tasters who swill morsels around in their mouths, and make postures of such cuisine hauteur that they don't seem to enjoy eating at all.

Nor do many of the chefs seem to enjoy cooking. That's where our worlds divide. The cult of cuisine is, well, just that – a cult of cuisine. It has become ubiquitous as entertainment, but it bears no resemblance to home fare and feeding the family.

For most of us, the name of the game is cookery. I'm a cook. I cook for many people. I am unpaid. I cook for love because of love. My secret ingredient is love. Cooking is not work for me, it is what I do after work. Although, by one of the serendipities of life, it has fallen into the realms of my work life for many years.

Once upon a time, seeing yet another food page featuring swanky recipes – highly stylised harissa-scented filo stacked with matsutake mushroom and king crab – created by chefs with PhDs in balsamic reduction sauces, I took courage and spoke to the editor. Instead of 101 ways to stuff a poussin, surely the readers needed 101 ways to embellish two-minute ramen noodles. He laughed and said that would be fine, if anyone had 101 ways in instant noodles.

Well, not quite 101, but in my years as a supporting mum, I told him, I had learned quite a lot about budget cooking coupled with ease and speed. Sadly, he did not take this as a hint for a pay rise but, instead, challenged me to write a pilot 'poverty food' column. This led to a series of weekly columns that proved immensely popular for many years.

And thus did my House of the Raising Sons come to live under a benign public gaze as I wrote about experimenting with new recipes and exploring all manner of culinary budget-juggling. What darling lab rats were those boys.

The House of the Raising Sons has changed since the first columns. The boys have grown up. 'Testosterone teen' grew into mellow young manhood and 'older boy' turned into an elegant and eloquent adult – almost between meals, so swift seems to have been the passage.

The House of the Raising Sons began by chance. As a supporting mum, my solution to knowing where my children were was to suggest to them that they bring their friends home to play after school. They did. Nice lads they brought, too. I always invited them to join us for dinner. They always stayed for dinner. In fact, they just stayed. Before I knew it, we were a crowd. It was no great extravagance to extend the family in this way. It was all about prudent budget cooking. I played the farmers' market.

What we lacked in material things we made up for in conversation, laughter and live music around the house. The somewhat cramped and down-at-heel kitchen was the heart of the house – and the place from which I watched the boys grow up.

Economic and cheap are not the same thing. No one has ever accused me of being cheap. I have exquisitely expensive tastes – characterised by an unerring instinct that drives me straight to price tags at which even Paris Hilton would blanch. But, in the food department, it is all about the quantity of quality. Some recipes require expensive ingredients such as smoked salmon, but not a lot. It is amazing how far a small amount of smoked salmon goes in delivering elegant flavour and perfume to a pasta dish. And so the boys have grown up as discerning eaters. They don't have to be steered away from fast food outlets since they genuinely prefer the good meals at home.

My recipes come from everyone and everywhere, word-of-mouth from friends and traded with e-pals on the Internet. Sometimes dishes in restaurants inspire me to go home and do my own interpretation. Then there are cookery books. I am a voracious collector of old country recipe books from street markets and second-hand shops, seeking in their musty pages insights into the honest economies of harder times. I revere grandmothers and country people with their tricks for saving or best exploiting limited and seasonal resources. Hence, many recipes are derived from timeless traditions or have been passed from cook to cook.

Then there are recipes invented according to the ingredients on hand – or developments of ideas that tickle the appetite, so to speak. Glut crops and bargain buys. The golden rule is that when you create a recipe that really works, write it down! My dog-eared handwritten personal recipe book is extremely precious to me.

The recipes herein have proven popular with readers, too. This second edition of *On a Shoestring – Recipes from the House of the Raising Sons* arrives by popular demand because it is tailor-made for recession proofing. It is a book about living really comfortably in hard times, about making each everyday meal something special and about making home the best place in the world to be. It is also a book for busy working parents by a busy working parent.

Most of the recipes serve from four to six people, but can be easily stretched to suit any number. You should not be intimidated by recipes, nor bound by them. Recipes are always evolving. Sometimes you make adjustments because of a lack of specific ingredients, or because you are in a certain mood for a bit more of this or less of that. Recipes are guidelines. They are not rules.

Conversion

....

Tablespoons are different.

When I started cooking in the USA, I insisted on using 'proper' Aussie tablespoons and insisting that they were 'proper tablespoons'. I was right in Australia – but wrong in the USA. It turns out that American tablespoons are smaller. They are 15 ml versus 20 ml for the Australian counterpart. Canadians have different ones, too. They use 15 ml while Britain uses a 17.7 ml spoon. Confused? Well, rightly so.

I dare to admit that I have used Aussie tablespoons when cooking from British and American recipes as well as those of my homeland. I also dare to admit that it never seemed to cause any great culinary catastrophe. As I have said and continue to say, recipes are not hard-and-fast rules. They are guidelines.

Nonetheless, what we all need in our kitchens are measuring implements that offer as many conversion alternatives as possible.

Here is a handy reference, just in case:

Abbreviations:

TSPN:	teaspoon
TBSPN:	tablespoon
C:	Celsius
F:	Fahrenheit
G:	gram
KG:	kilogram

Liquid or Volume Measures (approximate)				
Unit of measure	Equivalent measurement	Equivalent measurement	Decimal equivalent	Metric measurement
1 teaspoon		1/3 tablespoon	0.33 tablespoon	5 ml
1 tablespoon	1/2 fluid ounce	3 teaspoons	0.5 fluid ounce	15 ml, 15 cc
2 tablespoons	1 fluid ounce	1/8 cup, 6 teaspoons	0.125 cup	30 ml, 30 cc
1/4 cup	2 fluid ounces	4 tablespoons	0.25 cup	59 ml
1/3 cup	2 2/3 fluid ounces	5 tablespoons & 1 teaspoon	0.33 cup	79 ml
1/2 cup	4 fluid ounces	8 tablespoons	0.5 cup	118 ml
2/3 cup	5 1/3 fluid ounces	10 tablespoons & 2 teaspoons	0.67 cup	158 ml
3/4 cup	6 fluid ounces	12 tablespoons	0.75 cup	177 ml
7/8 cup	7 fluid ounces	14 tablespoons	0.875 cup	207 ml
1 cup	8 fluid ounces/ 1/2 pint	16 tablespoons	1.0 cup	237 ml
2 cups	16 fluid ounces/ 1 pint	32 tablespoons	2.0 cup	473 ml
4 cups	32 fluid ounces	1 quart	4.0 cup	946 ml
1 pint	16 fluid ounces/ 1 pint	32 tablespoons	1.0 pint	473 ml
2 pints	32 fluid ounces	1.0 quart	1.0 quart	946 ml 0.946 liters
8 pints	1 gallon/ 128 fluid ounces	4 quarts	1.0 gallon	3785 ml 3.78 liters
4 quarts	1 gallon/ 128 fluid ounces	8 pints	1.0 gallon	3785 ml 3.78 liters
1 liter	1.057 quarts			1000 ml
128 fluid ounces	1 gallon			3785 ml 3.78 liters

Dry or Weight Measurements (approximate)			
Unit of measure	Equivalent measure- ment	Decimal equivalent	Metric measurement
1 ounce	1/16 pound	0.0625 pound	30 grams(28.35 g)
2 ounces	1/8 pound	0.125 pound	55 grams
3 ounces	3/16 pound	0.1875 pound	85 grams
4 ounces	1/4 pound	0.25 pound	125 grams
8 ounces	1/2 pound	0.5 pound	240 grams
12 ounces	3/4 pound	0.75 pound	375 grams
16 ounces	1 pound	1.0 pound	454 grams
32 ounces	2 pounds	2.0 pounds	907 grams
1 kilogram	2.2 pounds/ 35.2 ounces		1000 grams

Temperature

° Fahrenheit	° Celsius (Centigrade)
32	0
212	100
250	140
300	150
325	160
350	180
375	190
400	200
425	220
450	230
475	240
500	260

US measurements (fluid)	Metric equivalent
1 teaspoon	5 milliliters
1 tablespoon	15 milliliters
$^{1}/_{4}$ cup	60 milliliters
$^{1}/_{2}$ cup	120 milliliters
$^{3}/_{4}$ cup	180 milliliters
1 cup	240 milliliters

US measurements (weight)	Metric equivalent
$^{1}/_{3}$ ounce	10 grams
$^{1}/_{2}$ ounce	15 grams
1 ounce	28 $^{1}/_{3}$ grams
4 ounces	114 grams
1 pound	464 grams

Weight measures

To convert:

– weight ounces into grams, multiply the ounces by 28.35
– grams into weight ounces, multiply the grams by 0.35

Soups to Warm the Cockles and Fill the Hollow Legs

And so the quest goes on – how to plump out the lean times? It's faintly ironic that the body's comfort needs of winter manage to give the pocket a bit of a rest. Then again, what's saved in the supermarket ends up being spent on the power bill.

There's no winning. But the managing is good enough for us in the House of the Raising Sons. Winter nights are spent bowing heads over aromatic bowls of steaming soups accompanied by loaves of fresh, crusty bread.

By the way, it's a good idea to keep the water from vegetables to use as vegetable stocks in winter but, if you haven't had the opportunity or foresight, then vegetable stock cubes do well.

Red Lentil Soup

It occurred to me, as I sliced through another loaf of rich wholemeal bread to serve with soup, that pulses are not so named for nothing. Come winter, they're the pulses of life.

Lentils, for example, are literally biblical in their nutritive antiquity. Not only are they cheap and wholesome sources of protein, minerals, fibre and B vitamins, but also they don't need dreary hours of pre-soaking. Just a good wash and pick-over. And they sustain the starving hordes most adequately.

There was not a solitary bottomless grizzle of 'what's the next course?' after I presented my pack of moveable, feasting males with this oh-so-easy soup for dinner.

4 TBSPN OLIVE OIL
3 LARGE ONIONS, FINELY SLICED
2 FAT CLOVES GARLIC, CRUSHED
8 CUPS VEGETABLE STOCK
500 G RED LENTILS
2 BAY LEAVES
1 TBSPN SOY SAUCE
2 TBSPN CHOPPED PARSLEY

Heat the oil in a large saucepan and fry the onions and garlic, stirring frequently, until they begin to caramelise. When light golden brown, add the stock and bring to the boil. Meanwhile, wash and pick over the lentils. Add to the boiling stock and, when the combination is boiling, reduce the heat to a good simmer and add the bay leaves. Cover and simmer for an hour before removing the bay leaves and adding the soy sauce and parsley. No further seasoning should be necessary.

Pumpkin Soup

This is a bargain basement soup. They don't come any cheaper – or any more sustaining. It is hard to beat such traditional, tasty fare.

1½ KG PUMPKIN
WATER AS REQUIRED
MILK AS REQUIRED
SALT, PEPPER AND GRATED
   NUTMEG TO TASTE

Skin, seed and cube the pumpkin and boil in just enough water to cover. Drain and puree. Add milk to desired consistency, season generously with salt, pepper and grated nutmeg and serve with fresh bread or toast.

Sweet Potato Soup

They're not always the most economical vegie, but this is one way to make glorious sweet potatoes go far.

2 LARGE ONIONS, CHOPPED
1 TBSPN BUTTER
1½ KG SWEET POTATO,
   PEELED AND CUBED
6 CUPS VEGETABLE STOCK
1 LARGE STICK CELERY
1 SMALL RED CAPSICUM
SALT, PEPPER AND GRATED
   NUTMEG TO TASTE

Lightly fry the onions in butter in a large saucepan, add the sweet potato and continue frying for five minutes. Add the stock and bring to the boil. Reduce heat to a good simmer and cook for about half an hour. Then add chopped celery and capsicum. Continue to cook for another half an hour. Add seasonings and puree the soup in a blender. Return to the pot and keep warm, but do not boil. If needed, dilute with a little milk or water.

Hearty Leek and Potato Soup

Simple is good. So long as I can remember this has been a family staple, a favourite of my father and superbly cooked by my mother. As with all the best old recipes, it is loved by every generation.

4 FAT LEEKS
3 MEDIUM POTATOES
1 LARGE ONION
2 TBSPN BUTTER
SALT AND BLACK PEPPER
   TO TASTE
4 CUPS CHICKEN OR
   VEGETABLE STOCK
1 CUP MILK
2 TBSPN CHOPPED PARSLEY

Wash leeks thoroughly. Slit tops down the centre for about a third of their length and wash the inside leaves under running water to remove all traces of dirt. Then complete the centre cut and slice into 1 cm or less pieces. Peel and slice potatoes into small cubes and chop onions finely. Melt the butter in a large saucepan and stir in the vegetables. Salt them and leave to sweat for about 15 minutes on a lowish heat before pouring in the stock and milk. Bring the lot to a simmer and cook for about half an hour, until the vegies are soft. Puree in a blender (or press through a sieve), store in the saucepan and heat when required. Serve with black pepper and chopped parsley.

A variation on this recipe is to use about four carrots instead of the potatoes. In this version, exclude the milk.

Thick Beetroot Soup

The boys aren't mad on beetroot but I am. This is one of the ways I charm and cajole the little sods into sharing my passion. It's so hearty and delicious, they don't seem to mind at all.

1 BUNCH BEETROOT
WATER AS REQUIRED
SALT TO TASTE
1 CLOVE GARLIC
A FEW DOLLOPS OF YOGHURT
CHOPPED PARSLEY AS REQUIRED
PEPPER TO TASTE

Wash beetroot, making sure the roots are not broken and there is still a small portion of stem where the leaves have been cut off (this prevents excessive 'bleeding' in the water). Place beetroot in a saucepan, cover with water, add the salt, pop a lid on top and boil until cooked. This is when the blade of a knife penetrates the beet easily. Remove from water. Do not discard water. Peel, trim and roughly chop the beetroot and put into a blender along with a crushed clove of garlic and some of the water. Blend, adding more beetroot water, until you have achieved a thick, soupy consistency. Then reheat the soup and serve in bowls topped with a big dollop of plain yoghurt, a generous sprinkling of parsley and lots of freshly ground black pepper.

Scots-style Barley Broth

The first of the House of the Raising Sons boys was born in Scotland so I sometimes cook nostalgia food to give him a sense of his origins. This is popular at Hogmanay, when wives like to know that their husbands' tummies are well lined before they whisk off to the whisky.

2 LAMB OR MUTTON SHANKS
   OR 1 KG NECK
WATER AS REQUIRED
SALT TO TASTE
2 TBSPN PEARL BARLEY
2 LEEKS
1 SMALL TURNIP
2 CARROTS
1 STICK CELERY
SALT AND PEPPER TO TASTE
CHOPPED PARSLEY AS REQUIRED

Trim meat, cover with cold water, add the salt, bring just to boiling point and turn down to simmer, skimming well. Wash the barley and add it to the meat. Simmer for at least an hour. Dice vegetables and add them to the pot. Simmer for another two hours or so. Lift the bones and carefully remove the meat, chopping it and returning it to the pot. Skim fat from the surface. Season with lots of black pepper and more salt, if wanted. Add the chopped parsley as you serve the soup.

Back-of-the-box Barley Soup

I really did take this recipe from the back of a box. A barley box in the United States. It has since undergone a few changes, but haven't we all?

500 G LEAN MINCE
OIL AS REQUIRED
1 LARGE ONION, FINELY CHOPPED
3 CLOVES GARLIC, CRUSHED
1 TIN TOMATOES, CHOPPED
1 CUP BARLEY, RINSED
1 STICK CELERY, CHOPPED
1 CARROT, CHOPPED
2 BEEF STOCK CUBES
1/2 TSPN BASIL LEAVES
1 BAY LEAF
1 TSPN CHILI POWDER
9 CUPS WATER
SALT AND PEPPER TO TASTE
1 SMALL PACK FROZEN CHOPPED
    MIXED VEGETABLES

Brown the meat in a little oil and add onion and garlic, cooking until onion is tender. Then simply stir in all the remaining ingredients, except the frozen vegetables. Bring to the boil, skim, reduce heat to simmer, cover and cook for about an hour, stirring occasionally. Add frozen vegetables. Cook for another 10 minutes or so until vegetables are tender. If necessary, add more water. This soup thickens on standing and is even better the next day. Serve with chunks of crusty bread.

Egg and Lemon Soup

I learned this recipe years ago from a cherished friend in Greece. We were desperately broke, but it didn't feel that way when it came to eating. The recipe has been a cheap standby ever since – a way to feel good when times are lean.

1 CUP RICE
8 CUPS PLAIN CHICKEN STOCK
SALT TO TASTE
3 EGGS
JUICE OF 1 LEMON

Cook rice in the boiling stock. Salt to taste. In a good-sized bowl, thoroughly beat eggs with lemon juice and, still beating, slowly pour in about two cups of the broth. Add this mixture to the hot soup, stirring well, and then cover the pot and let it stand for about five minutes away from the heat before serving.

Oriental Mushroom Soup

I have tried many variations on the mushroom theme in order to ensure lads are properly nourished. This is a beauty, and divinely quick and easy.

50 G CHICKEN BREAST,
  FINELY SHREDDED
1¹/₂ TSPN CORNFLOUR
2 TBSPN WATER
50 G MUSHROOMS, FINELY SLICED
6 CUPS HOT STOCK (WATER WITH
  A VEGETABLE CUBE)
2 TSPN LIGHT SOY SAUCE
SALT TO TASTE
A FEW SPRING ONIONS,
  FINELY CHOPPED

In a bowl mix the chicken with the cornflour and water. Place mushrooms in the hot stock and cook about five minutes before adding the chicken. Simmer for about five more minutes until the chicken is white and the soup slightly thickened. Add the soy sauce, salt and spring onions and serve.

Corn Chowder

One of the quickest, easiest, most economical and substantial soups in the world. It's an American classic, although this version is a hybrid.

2 LEAN RASHERS OF BACON FINELY
  CHOPPED (OR 1 TSPN SOY
  BACON BITS FOR VEGETARIANS)
1 MEDIUM ONION, FINELY CHOPPED
2 TBSPN BUTTER
2 LARGE YELLOW-FLESH POTATOES,
  PEELED AND DICED
1 CARROT, ALSO PEELED AND EVEN
  MORE FINELY DICED
1/2 CUP WATER
1 420 G (17 OZ) CAN CREAMED CORN
2 CUPS MILK
SALT AND BLACK PEPPER

Heat a large saucepan and cook the bacon pieces until they are crispy, then add onion and butter and cook until the onion is soft and beginning to brown. Add potato, carrot and water and simmer until vegetables are thoroughly tender. Then, add all the other ingredients and bring the chowder to hot but not boiling. Serve with chunks of fresh bread.

Fairly Classic Minestrone

The biggest drawback of being the big-family little-budget cook is the eternal relentlessness of it all. All the best cheap tucker is labour-intensive and, after a long day's work, there are nights when cooking the dinner looms like a mountain with no cup of coffee at the top. Oh for a night off.

Well, it can be arranged – with foresight and effort. It's the old hearty soup trick.

Like curries, some soups thrive on a night's rest. They achieve fullness and flavour if given twenty-four hours' snooze in the fridge. Of all such soups, minestrone is our family favourite – probably because the family consists of huge, hollow-bodied boys who want seconds even if you've fed them half a sheep.

Minestrone is substantial. It's also nourishing, filled with vitamins, fibre and trace minerals of beans and vegetables. And it's economical, being a perfect vehicle for all manner of vegetable remnants in the end-of-the-week fridge.

The rule for minestrone is to use whatever vegetables you have in whatever proportion you have them. The addition of beans and pasta creates the eventual balance anyway. So be not afraid of improvisation.

BEANS – 250 G MIXED ITALIAN
 DRIED BEANS SOAKED
 OVERNIGHT AND BOILED IN
 SALTY WATER UNTIL TENDER,
 OR 250 G RED KIDNEY BEANS
 TREATED IN THE SAME WAY OR,
 SIMILARLY, HARICOT BEANS,
 OR A LARGE CAN OF
 PRE-PREPARED RED
 KIDNEY BEANS
1 LARGE ONION, FINELY DICED
2 CLOVES GARLIC, CRUSHED
2 RED PEPPERS, IN SMALL CUBES
1/4 CABBAGE, CHOPPED
OLIVE OIL AS REQUIRED
1 SMALL TUB TOMATO PASTE OR
 TINNED TOMATOES BLENDED
6 CUPS STOCK
SOME CAULIFLOWER FLORETS
200 G MACARONI OR BROKEN-UP
 SPAGHETTI
SALT AND PEPPER TO TASTE
PINCH OF SUGAR
SPRINKLE OF CHOPPED PARSLEY
GRATED CHEESE (IDEALLY
 PARMESAN) AS REQUIRED

Having prepared and drained the beans, place the onion, garlic, peppers and cabbage in warm olive oil in a heavy-based saucepan and sweat, covered, for about 15 minutes. Mix in tomato, stock and cauliflower or other faster-cooking vegetables. Stew on medium-high heat for 45 minutes before adding beans. Continue to cook for another 45 minutes, then add pasta and let it cook for 15 minutes, adding salt, pepper, a pinch of sugar and more stock or water if necessary. When reheating to serve, add chopped parsley and sprinkle with parmesan.

In times when slavery

has been abolished...

still prevalent is...

the slave to love...

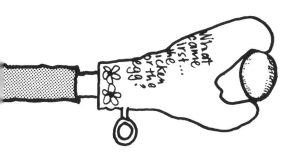

An Ova View

....

The good thing about having a few chickens in the back yard is that when all else runs out, there will be eggs. My four little chooks are, like most females, sturdily productive and dependable. Year in, year out, they scratch away in their corner, they fluff in the dust, they cluck contentedly and they recycle all the household scraps into lovely fresh googies.

Heaven only knows how old they are now. In chook years, they must be decidedly geriatric. But still they're working girls. And for one who lives in a house overwhelmed by males, they provide the only immediate female company.

There have been times when the heavy, often raucous nature of the male bonding games in the House of the Raising Sons has driven me desperate for some solace from my own kind. I've crept into the garden and talked to the chookies. Hens are not marvellous conversationalists, but they're quite good listeners. And they do make comforting noises of acknowledgment. A soft cluck here and there. A compassionate 'cor?' It's remarkable how soothing and therapeutic they can be – and giving.

Scratch Frittata

During those times when the food seems to have vanished way before it should have and the fridge is left with a random and seemingly useless assortment of bits and pieces, the bonus of a nice stash of eggs can turn a scratch meal into a scrumptious dinner. The Italians have quite a fancy name for the resulting dish – frittata. It's a sort of quiche-like omelette. Served with a crispy salad and some fresh bread, it's a proud meal made from humble odds and ends. Don't be limited by the vegetables I have suggested for this dish. You can cook broccoli, peas, cauliflower or almost any vegetable and incorporate it into this recipe. It helps if you have a frypan that will go in the oven.

6 SPRING ONIONS OR 1 MEDIUM ONION, CHOPPED
3 CLOVES GARLIC, CRUSHED
3 TBSPN OLIVE OIL
1 LARGE RED CAPSICUM, IN FINE STRIPS
1 ZUCCHINI, SLICED
12 OR SO GREEN BEANS, SLICED
1 LARGE TOMATO, CHOPPED
SALT AND FRESHLY GROUND BLACK PEPPER TO TASTE
2 TBSPN CHOPPED PARSLEY
2 TSPN DRIED BASIL (OR 1 TBSPN FRESH)
12 EGGS
1 CUP GRATED CHEDDAR CHEESE

In a large ovenproof pan, fry the onions and garlic in the oil until the onion softens. Add the other vegetables and fry until they are cooked through. Allow them to cool a little before seasoning generously with salt, pepper and herbs. Beat the eggs lightly and then combine together with the vegetables. Return to the heat and cook for a few minutes, lifting the sides and running the egg mixture under so that it is evenly distributed. Sprinkle the cheese over the top and then place the whole pan in a medium-hot (200°C) oven for about 15–20 minutes.

Tortilla – Spanish Omelette

I have cooked this a squillion times. Not only does it content the hungry hordes but it makes for the most wonderful leftovers. School lunches were never better.

2 LARGE ONIONS, FINELY CHOPPED
2 LARGE POTATOES, FINELY CHOPPED OR GRATED
1/2 CUP OLIVE OIL
6–10 EGGS
SALT AND BLACK PEPPER TO TASTE
1 CUP OF GRATED CHEDDAR CHEESE
A FEW SLICES OF HAM, CHOPPED

Gently fry the onions and potatoes in the oil in a wide frying pan. When the vegetables are golden, lift them out on a slotted spatula so the oil drizzles back into the pan. Beat the eggs, season generously and add the vegetables along with the cheese and the ham. Mix well and return the lot to the pan to cook slowly. When a crust begins to form on the sides and the bottom, pop the frypan under the grill to brown the top. Let the whole thing rest for 10–15 minutes before slicing it in wedges and serving with a crisp, green salad.

No Escaping Eggsotic Meals

Of course it all looked very spruce and tidy when I lumbered in from the airport and made a mess unpacking pressies in the back room. But I wasn't fooled. I knew they'd finished only moments before after a frenzy of last-minute cleaning. I didn't mind. That's par for the course when boys have been batching. It could have been worse. Like the salami stains my unruly uni mates once inflicted on my parents' living room walls when they were overseas.

What mystified me was what the boys ate during my two-week absence from the House of the Raising Sons. I know what it wasn't. Eggs.

I've never seen so many eggs. Clearly the chooks were relieved of them as a last-minute thought, too, though the boys indignantly insisted they had collected the eggs daily as per my instructions. It's just that, er, well, they hadn't really felt like eating eggs. Well, um, on second thoughts, they had eaten lots of eggs but the chooks laid eggs faster than they could eat them. Obviously, each chook was laying six eggs a day.

So for the next few days there was some intensive egg-eating to work through the googie surfeit – and, since I'd just been in beautiful Bali peering over the shoulders of accomplished young cooks turning out exquisite and complex repasts on nothing more than a couple of portable gas rings, it was Indonesian egg dishes in a big way.

It's so much quicker and easier for us than it is for them. They don't have food processors. They do all their grinding and paste-making in very flat stone mortar and pestle utensils.

These dishes are a wonderful variation for us. They're quite different from our normal egg meals yet equally simple. The boys couldn't say which of the dishes they liked best – but approvingly wolfed down every scrap and commented that at least I'd spent my time in Bali constructively, so maybe I'd earned the suntan!

Coconut Omelette

2 SPRING ONIONS
1 FRESH RED CHILI
(OR ½ TSPN CHILI POWDER)
1 CLOVE GARLIC
DASH OF WATER
2 HEAPED TBSPN DESICCATED
COCONUT
SALT TO TASTE
6 MEDIUM EGGS
2 TBSPN VEGETABLE OIL

Clean and roughly chop the spring onions and seed the chili. Then whiz with the garlic in a food processor, adding a dash of water to help it turn into a smooth paste. Add the coconut, some salt, and lastly the eggs. Give them a thorough beating and then pour into a hot, oiled large frypan or wok. Tip the mixture so it's evenly spread and cook on a medium heat until the omelette is golden brown on the bottom. Now you have to turn it over and brown the other side. In my large frypan, I find it easier to slice it into portions to do this. When the omelette is well browned on both sides, remove it and slice into strips. Serve it with rice and salad or on its own.

Sweet Soy Omelette

1 SMALL ONION, FINELY CHOPPED
2 SMALL RED CHILIES,
FINELY CHOPPED
2 TBSPN VEGETABLE OIL
4 EGGS
2 TSPN SWEET SOY SAUCE
(AVAILABLE AT
SUPERMARKETS, OR YOU CAN
MAKE IT BY USING DARK SOY
OR MUSHROOM SOY AND
ADDING A TEASPOON OF SOFT
BROWN SUGAR)

Fry the onion and chilies in oil until well cooked, then beat together the eggs and soy sauce and pour into the pan, shaking well to amalgamate the ingredients and create an even spread. Cook on a medium heat steadily until the whole omelette is firm and brown on the bottom. Serve in slices or strips, again with rice or on its own.

Eggs with Piquant Tomato Sauce

A variation on the egg theme is boiled eggs served in a spicy, piquant sauce. This is better as a side dish with a curry meal, accompanied by rice.

4 SPRING ONIONS
2 CLOVES GARLIC
2 RED CHILIES (OR 1 TSPN CHILI POWDER)
VEGETABLE OIL AS REQUIRED
450 G CAN TOMATOES, PUREED
2 TBSPN DARK SOY SAUCE
1 CUP WATER
SALT TO TASTE
6–8 HARD-BOILED EGGS, PEELED

Grind up the spring onions, garlic and chili in a food processor or mortar and pestle with a little oil to make a smooth paste and then fry in a lightly oiled saucepan for a couple of minutes. Then add the tomatoes, soy sauce, water and salt and cook on a medium heat for about 10 minutes before adding the eggs. Coat them well and simmer for a few minutes before serving.

Raffenio Egg Fries

This is a Greek version of egg and chips.

4 LARGE POTATOES
1/2 CUP OLIVE OIL (OR OLIVE OIL DILUTED WITH ANOTHER VEGETABLE OIL)
6 TO 8 EGGS
GENEROUS PINCH MIXED HERBS
SALT AND PEPPER TO TASTE

Peel and cut potatoes into chips. In a wide frying pan, sizzle in the hot oil until golden. Beat eggs in a bowl with the herbs and, when fries are perfect, pour the egg mixture over and around the potatoes. Turn the heat down and let the eggs firm up, sprinkling them with salt and lots of freshly ground black pepper. Serve immediately.

Shirley Temple

One very popular standby dish is this classic fried bread and egg number –
known in my family, for some mysterious reason, as Shirley Temple.

SLICES OF WHITE OR
WHOLEMEAL BREAD AT LEAST
THREE DAYS OLD
BUTTER OR MARGARINE
AS REQUIRED
EGGS (ONE FOR EACH SLICE
OF BREAD)

De-crust the bread and cut a neat 4 cm hole in the middle. Melt a generous dollop of butter in a large frying pan and, when it's sizzling, add the slices of bread and the bits from the middles. Fry until golden crispy brown on both sides and then care-fully crack an egg into the holes in each slice of bread. Sizzle until the base firms and then smoothly flip over and firm the egg white on the other side. Remove from the frying pan while the yolk is still runny and serve quickly with the middles, salt and lots of freshly ground black pepper.

French Toast

Not just a breakfast of the gods (or spoiled-rotten lads) but a divine dessert.

SLICES OF WHITE BREAD AT
LEAST THREE DAYS OLD
EGGS AS REQUIRED
MILK AS REQUIRED
BUTTER OR MARGARINE
AS REQUIRED
CINNAMON AND SUGAR
TO TASTE

De-crust the bread. Mix beaten eggs and an equal amount of milk in a bowl. Soak bread in the mixture. Melt butter in a large frying pan and, when it's sizzling, fry the soaked bread pieces on both sides until they are golden brown. Serve sprinkled with cinnamon and sugar.

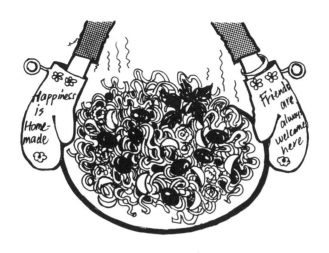

Pasta and Rice Ammunition

Sending out the big accounts all at once makes as much sense as putting all the telly news services on at the same time. It strips us poor consumers of liberty of lifestyle. It harnesses us all to mass belt-tightening – and scratching around in the pantry to use up all those cunningly purchased specials and just-in-case items.

Things in the House of the Raising Sons were particularly dire on one occasion. Telstra's dispassionate computer count of the teenage phoneaholia in the place was the last crippling straw. Who are all these kids on mobiles? And how can boys rack up an average of fifteen calls a day? Daily frenzies of networking, all concluded with the words 'I'll ring you back'!

They talk about drugs and pokie addiction but where are the rehab and support groups for the phoneaholics and their long-suffering families?

These things I pondered as I scrabbled grumpily through the cupboards looking for Shoestring inspiration and with relief spied the pasta and the rice.

Fail-safe Rice

This technique was taught to me by a sad, homesick Thai girl, most inappropriately named Fun. It's really the absorption method. Fun never washed the rice before cooking. I sometimes do, if it looks dusty. Usually the Thai Jasmine rice I bulk-buy economically in Asian supermarkets (the ten-kilogram bags come in sturdy, re-useable shopping bags) is as clean as it's aromatic. Expensive basmati also cooks perfectly the Fun way.

For perfect Fun rice, the secret is two cups of rice to three cups of cold water. Place the rice and water in a heavy-bottomed stainless-steel or enamel saucepan and cover with a well-fitting lid. Bring to a rapid boil when the lid is rattling or when a touch of froth shows at the rim. Do not, repeat, DO NOT, lift the lid!

Turn off the heat and let the rice stand for twenty minutes to half an hour. Then lift the lid and, using a fork, prongs vertical, tease the rice thoroughly to separate it. Serve immediately or replace the lid, leaving a little crack for steam, and serve later. Rice retains its heat well and loses nothing in texture.

she braced herself against the elements ...

Brown Rice Casserole

You'd be pushing it to get a cheaper family dinner than this.

4 CUPS HOT VEGETABLE STOCK
2¹/₃ CUPS ROUND-GRAIN
  BROWN RICE
6 ONIONS, SLICED
2 TBSPN MARGARINE
SALT AND BLACK PEPPER
  TO TASTE
400 G GRATED CHEDDAR CHEESE

Bring the stock and rice to the boil in a large, tight-lidded saucepan and then turn down the heat and let it simmer for about 40 minutes until all the stock is absorbed. Fry the onions in margarine until they are beginning to caramelise. When the rice is cooked, grease a casserole dish and press half the rice into the bottom. Cover with half the onions, season, then repeat with the rest of the rice and the rest of the onions. Press it down and cover with grated cheese. Bake in a 180–200°C oven until the cheese has melted into the rice and begun to brown. Serve hot with a salad.

Nasi Brenda

This is another firm family favourite, a sensationally healthy sort of fried rice dish that is nice eaten hot or cold.

2¹/₃ CUPS ROUND-GRAIN
  BROWN RICE
4 CUPS HOT WATER
2 MEDIUM ONIONS, CHOPPED
4 TBSPN OLIVE OIL
GARLIC AS REQUIRED (SALT-
  PICKLED GARLIC CLOVES ARE
  SUPERB IN THIS DISH)
250 G MUSHROOMS
A LITTLE CHILI (POWDERED
  OR FRESH)
1 TBSPN CURRY POWDER
A GENEROUS HANDFUL OF
  CHOPPED PARSLEY
1 TBSPN CHOPPED BASIL
ABOUT 3 CUPS CHOPPED
  VEGETABLE/S OF CHOICE

Cook rice as in the previous recipe. Meanwhile, in your largest frying pan, fry onions in olive oil. When they are translucent, add as much chopped garlic as you like, then the sliced mushrooms, the chili, the curry powder, and the parsley and basil. Separately, steam the vegetables of your choice. Pumpkin in 2 cm cubes is terrific. So are cauliflower florets. Drain the cooked vegetables. Mix the rice into the onion mixture and add the vegetables, tossing them through thoroughly. Serve with sweet mango pickle and/or chili sambal.

Fried Rice

Leftovers heaven. There are few rules here.

1 LARGE ONION, FINELY CHOPPED
2.5 CM FRESH GINGER, GRATED
3 CLOVES GARLIC, CRUSHED
1–2 TBSPN VEGETABLE OIL
ASSORTED VEGETABLES OR
   LEFTOVERS – BUT, IDEALLY:
   1 CARROT IN JULIENNE STRIPS
   OR FINELY DICED
   1 CUP OF PEAS, FRESH OR
   FROZEN
   SMALL PORTION OF CABBAGE,
   FINELY DICED
   A COUPLE OF CAULIFLOWER
   SEGMENTS CUT INTO
   SMALL FLORETS
3 SLICES OF HAM, FINELY DICED
   (OR, FOR VEGETARIANS,
   A SCANT HANDFUL OF SOYA
   BACON CHIPS)
A FEW DASHES OF SOY SAUCE
2 EGGS

In a big frying pan or wok, fry onion, ginger and garlic in the oil, then add the assorted vegetables and stir-fry until cooked but not soft, adding the ham or bacon bits towards the end. Carefully tip in the rice, stirring the ingredients together thoroughly. Soy sauce may be added at this point to give a little colour and saltiness. Beat the eggs separately and, using a small frypan, fry small amounts of egg into very thin omelettes which can be cut into fine strips and used to garnish the rice. If you have access to fresh beensprouts, wash them and toss them through at the end.

Chicken Paella

The idea that the simplicity of holiday shacks gives mum a domestic rest is a man-made myth. When you remove the family to a rented beach shack, mum is removed from all those things she's spent years setting up to make the cooking process quick and easy.

Suddenly she's back in the domestic dark ages and the only thing restful is the view. While dad and kids roar off to do all those lovely, bonding holiday outdoor things, mum's usual role is to come to terms with the new environment.

This means unearthing a rusty 1950s can-opener, a pile of dented aluminium saucepans, chipped cups and plates, an amazingly kitsch souvenir cruet, half a set of 1960s storage canisters and, joy of joys, an old but working electric frypan.

Oh, how she'll caress its grease-ingrained lid. What the bonding dad is doing with the kids is nothing compared to the deep emotional link mum is forging with the trusty frypan. Believe me.

It's amazing what you can cook in electric frypans. You can even roast a rabbit, if you're so inclined. But when on holidays, easy is the way to go. And one of the niftiest ways to feed the well-exercised and subsequently urgently ravenous family is with this cheap and low-effort Spanish-style repast.

It's a holiday standby anywhere, this one. The boys of the House of the Raising Sons, imbued with hearty appetites on holidays or not, give it big ticks in the hearty summer meal repertoire. It's also fairly flexible, one of those recipes which will accommodate endless variations on ingredients. So this is the way I usually do it – but don't feel restricted.

3 LARGE ONIONS, CHOPPED
MEDIUM-FINE
3 CLOVES GARLIC
1 TSPN GRATED GINGER
1 TSPN TURMERIC
1/3 CUP OLIVE OIL
2 KG CHICKEN PIECES
1 RED CAPSICUM,
FINELY CHOPPED
1 CUP DRY SHERRY
2 CUPS WATER
SALT AND BLACK PEPPER
TO TASTE
2 CUPS RICE
1 CUP COOKED PEAS

Fry the onions, garlic, ginger and turmeric in hot olive oil until onions soften, then add the chicken and cook on both sides until it begins to turn golden. Add the capsicum and fry a little longer before pouring on the sherry and water. Bring to the boil, adding the pepper and salt. Then add the rice, cover securely and cook on a medium-low heat until the rice has absorbed all the liquid, adding more water if necessary. Add the cooked peas, mix well, check the seasoning, cover and leave on low for another 15 minutes or so – or until the crowd turns up to eat. You can turn it off and reheat it. Serve with a crisp salad.

Rice Balls

A nifty little treat. Nice on the dinner plate and a whiz in the finger food department.

3 CUPS COOKED RICE
1 CUP GRATED CHEDDAR CHEESE
1 TBSPN CHOPPED DRIED
   PARSLEY
2 TSPN CHOPPED DRIED CHIVES
1 TSPN PAPRIKA
DASH CHILI POWDER
1 TBSPN PLAIN FLOUR
SALT AND FRESHLY GROUND
   BLACK PEPPER TO TASTE
1 EGG, BEATEN WITH MILK
DRY BREADCRUMBS
   AS REQUIRED
OIL AND BUTTER
   AS REQUIRED

In a bowl, mix everything except the egg, milk and breadcrumbs. When the ingredients are well-amalgamated, press into 3-cm diameter balls, dip into the egg and milk, roll in breadcrumbs and fry in a hot mixture of half oil and butter.

— Maxwell.

Mum's the word.

Rice Pie

In lieu of conventional vegetables, this is a handsome and delectable accompaniment to meat dishes, roast chicken or even fish.

1 TBSPN BUTTER
2 EGGS, BEATEN
1 TBSPN CHOPPED CHIVES
SALT, PEPPER AND PAPRIKA
　TO TASTE
2 CUPS FRESHLY COOKED
　JASMINE RICE

Blend butter, eggs, chives and seasonings into the warm rice and then press it into a well-greased pyrex or casserole dish.

FILLING:
2–3 LARGE ONIONS,
　FINELY CHOPPED
2 TBSPN BUTTER
250 G MUSHROOMS, SLICED
1/4 CAULIFLOWER, FINELY SLICED
200 G CHEDDAR CHEESE, GRATED

Fry the onions in the butter until golden. Add the mushrooms and soften. Blanch the cauliflower in boiling water. Cover the rice with half the grated cheese, then place half the fried onion and mushroom mix on top of that, then the cauliflower, another layer of cheese and finally the rest of the onion mix. Press everything down firmly.

TOPPING:
2 EGGS
SALT AND PEPPER TO TASTE
DASH OF CHILI POWDER
1/2 CUP CREAM
1 TOMATO, SLICED

Mix eggs, seasonings and cream and pour evenly over the top of the pie. Put in a 180°C oven for about an hour, until the centre is firm. Remove from oven and place tomato rings decoratively on top. Return to oven for 10 more minutes before taking out, cooling a little while, then slicing and serving.

Balinese Noodles: Mie Villa Indah

Once tasted, a 'must cook' dish. I nearly drove the girls mad at Villa Indah in Bali while I loitered around the kitchen learning how they cooked it.

TWO-MINUTE NOODLES
(ONE PACK PER PERSON)
2 TBSPN TOMATO SAUCE
8 CLOVES GARLIC, CRUSHED
1 SMALL ONION, FINELY CHOPPED
1 TSPN GRATED GINGER
PINCH OF TURMERIC
VEGETABLE OIL AS REQUIRED
1 SMALL RED CAPSICUM,
FINELY SLICED
1 CUP SLICED GREEN BEANS
1 TOMATO, CHOPPED
1 CUP FINELY SLICED CABBAGE
1 SPRING ONION, CHOPPED
1 CHICKEN STOCK CUBE
1 TBSPN SWEET SOY SAUCE
1 CUP FINELY SLICED COOKED
CHICKEN
1 CUCUMBER, SLICED
2 TOMATOES, SLICED
1 RED CHILI, CHOPPED
EXTRA CHILI AND SOY SAUCE
IF REQUIRED

Cook the noodles, drain, mix roughly with the tomato sauce. Leave to cool completely. Turn occasionally to ensure they separate well. While they are cooling, fry the garlic, onion, ginger and turmeric in a little vegetable oil. Add the capsicum, beans and tomato, and stir-fry until the beans begin to become tender. Add the remainder of the vegetables, the stock cube and half the soy. Continue to cook until cabbage softens. Add chicken and noodles. Drizzle through the last of the sweet soy and serve with sliced cucumber and tomato as a side garnish. You may like to add a simple sambal for extra spice. Chop a hot chili and put it in a small bowl of light soy sauce to be spooned on the noodles for extra piquancy.

Two-minute Dinner Party

This very civilised Asian-Australian way of embellishing two-minute noodles has long been an easy working weekend lunch around the House of the Raising Sons. But there have been impromptu moments when circumstances rule that extra people must be fed. They never fail to be impressed that such a 'scratch' meal can be so attractive and appetising.

1 PACKET TWO-MINUTE NOODLES PER PERSON, COOKED AS PER PACKET INSTRUCTIONS

Prepare a large platter to place in the centre of the table. Arrange upon it in neat piles:

CHOPPED BOILED EGGS
SHREDDED LETTUCE
BLANCHED BEAN SPROUTS
DICED HAM
SLICED CHILIES

Spag Bol

We had a food fight in the House of the Raising Sons – and we didn't make a mess at all.

This is because it was more of a heated debate than a fight. And it is really hard to say who won, since we all think we are right.

Spaghetti bolognaise, you see, is one of those things about which many people have very strong opinions. Everyone has their own special way of cooking it. Its Italian origins are long lost in its domestic ubiquity.

The big spag yike began when one of my Internet friends e-mailed me his secret bolognaise recipe. It required no wine. It was very different from my recipe. And my recipe is different from the improvisations adopted by the assorted boys, all of whom have evolved some sort of version of a bolognaise. As occasional cooks, they are inordinately proud of their expertise. They think their version is superior to all forerunners.

The only point of agreement we could reach was that 'spag bol' has turned into a free-for-all dish. It is a way in which any cook can express their person-ality. I know some cooks who twice fry and drain the mince. Others who omit tomato. One who excludes garlic. One who uses Rosella tomato sauce. They're all different recipes by the same name.

So I'm going on the record. I have been cooking spag bol this way since my student days – and it is such a terrific sauce that I have only changed it when I have run out of necessary ingredients. Even so, it works. I used port wine once – and it was terrific.

The important thing about this version is that it stretches the meat while remaining a meaty dish. It goes further. It feeds, it freezes, it's nice on rice, on toast . . .

2 MEDIUM ONIONS,
   FINELY CHOPPED
OLIVE OIL AS REQUIRED
3 CLOVES GARLIC, CRUSHED
1 KG LEAN MINCE
$1/2$ CUP RED WINE
1 CARTON TOMATO PASTE
1 LARGE CAN TOMATOES,
   CHOPPED WITH JUICE
1 SMALL CAN CONDENSED
   TOMATO SOUP
1 HEAPED TSPN VEGEMITE
   (OPTIONAL)
2 TSPN MIXED HERBS (FRENCH
   HERBES DE PROVENCE IF YOU
   HAVE THEM)
$1/4$ TSPN SUGAR
DASH OF CHILI
SALT AND FRESHLY GROUND
   BLACK PEPPER TO TASTE
1 TBSPN FINELY CHOPPED
   FRESH PARSLEY

Soften onions in olive oil until they are translucent. Add garlic and fry a little longer. Add mince and stir well to brown. Add the wine and continue to stir and brown. Then throw in all the other ingredients except the parsley, stir well and put on a medium heat to cook steadily for about an hour, until the oil comes to the top and the sauce is thick and rich. Stir in the parsley. Serve with the pasta of your choice accompanied by lots of grated parmesan, romano or sharp cheddar cheese. A tart side salad is a nice addition.

Orchard Pasta

This is probably the most refreshing pasta dish in pasta world. It's a huge hit with vegetarians. The secret to its flavour is the fresh tomato. No canned substitutes in this recipe. And, of course, the orange zest is the big fresh flavour.

3 YELLOW-FLESH POTATOES, COOKED

1/4 HEAD OF CAULIFLOWER, BROKEN INTO FLORETTES

1/3 CUP COLD-PRESSED OLIVE OIL

2 CLOVES GARLIC, CRUSHED

2 MEDIUM-SIZED ZUCCHINI IN THICK JULIENNE SLICES

1 KG RIPE FRESH TOMATOES, SKINNED AND CHOPPED

3 OR 4 MIDDLE-SIZED MUSHROOMS, SLICED

1 GREEN CHILI, SLICED FINELY

2 ORANGES (JUICE OF BOTH AND FINELY GRATED ZEST OF ONE)

CHOPPED PARSLEY

SALT AND FRESHLY GROUND BLACK PEPPER

Boil the potatoes, then cool, peel and slice. Cook the cauliflower until just done. In a deep frypan, heat the oil and sizzle the garlic with the zucchini, allowing the zucchini to gain just a little colour before throwing in the tomatoes. Give them a few minutes to warm through and soften and then add the mushrooms, cauliflower, potatoes, orange juice and orange zest and chili. Simmer for 10 to 15 minutes. Cook 500 g pasta of choice. I like spiralli for this dish but it doesn't matter. When the pasta is cooked, drain it and then blend it into the sauce and serve. A little parsley and grated cheddar cheese is rather nice on top.

Salmon Pasta

A small amount of smoked salmon can go a very long way. This luscious and fancy dish does not break the budget. If asparagus is in season, then it is salmon and asparagus. If asparagus is expensive, replace it with one and a half cups of frozen peas.

1/4 CUP OLIVE OIL
2 CLOVES GARLIC, CRUSHED
2 BUNCHES ASPARAGUS
 CHOPPED AND COOKED (OR 1
 1/2 CUPS COOKED FROZEN
 PEAS)
1 TBSPN BRANDY
300 G TUB RICOTTA OR LIGHT
 PHILADELPHIA CREAM CHEESE
1 CUP HOT WATER
200–250 G SMOKED SALMON,
 DICED
3 TBSPN FINELY CHOPPED MIXED
 FRESH HERBS (PARSLEY, BASIL,
 OREGANO, THYME)
SALT AND FRESHLY GROUND
 BLACK PEPPER
1 FINELY CHOPPED GREEN CHILI
 (OPTIONAL)
400 G ANGEL HAIR PASTA
PARMESAN (OPTIONAL)

In a deep frying pan, warm the oil, cook the garlic gently then add the asparagus (or peas), warm well and add the brandy. Stir to evaporate and then add the ricotta (or phily), mixing well. Incorporate the water so there is a smoothish consistency. Throw in the salmon and then the herbs and seasoning. Try not to boil the mix, it will shrink the salmon bits. Mix the hot, cooked pasta in the sauce and serve promptly – with or without added parmesan cheese.

Pasta Broccoli

What? Me worry? Why should I? I was only going away for one night. Each and every one of the boys gave his absolute assurance that everything would be all right in a motherless House of the Raising Sons.

They're big boys, they insisted. Responsible. Everything would be okay. After all, what could go wrong in just one night?

So I didn't pester them with phone calls. Just one to check the puppy had been fed and there was fresh water out for dogs and chooks. Everything was under control, they insisted. Have a nice time, Mum. Relax.

So I did – and drove home next day feeling a wondrous sense of well-being in the radiant spring countryside, never suspecting the price I had paid for that one night out of town.

Nobody knew how the shelves had fallen off the wall. None of the boys had been in the kitchen at the time when this massive calamity had occurred.

But they had done a good job of clearing up all the breakages and had even thought of some much improved designs for replacement shelving.

If I could just find some woodworking genius to execute them. Mysterious. Even the puppy was somewhere else.

I had no sooner surveyed the shambles of jars and storage pots that had survived the crash than the youngest teen rocked up from behind and surrounded me in a bear hug.

'It's okay. He put ice on it,' volunteered his brother.

'It's not bad, Mum. Doesn't hurt much,' added the towering baby of the family.

As he released me, I saw his growing shiner and the cut above his eye.

There wasn't a fight exactly. 'Some dude' was the person who did it. The babe was only trying to defend one of his mates. And the dude had said he was sorry afterwards.

Everyone was friends now, so it was all right. Please don't fuss. That the puppy had demolished the last of my surviving pot plants and every light in the house had clearly been left on overnight seemed neither here nor there after my other homecoming surprises. The boys were hungry and so was I.

Clearing a path through the displaced kitchen paraphernalia, I hunted through the fridge for dinner.

'Oh, weren't we supposed to eat that?' they asked of the previous evening's intended meal.

If ever there was a tax to maternal ingenuity, this was it. But all the negatives of the calamitous homecoming were assuaged as we soothed body and soul with one of the simplest of shortcut dinners.

The trick to remember is that pasta is so versatile it goes with almost any-thing – in this case, a bunch of bargain broccoli.

4 GARLIC CLOVES, CRUSHED
1/2 CUP GOOD OLIVE OIL
1 BUNCH OF BROCCOLI, CUT INTO FLORETS AND LIGHTLY STEAMED
SALT AND FRESHLY GROUND BLACK PEPPER TO TASTE
PINCH CHILI POWDER
1 CUP GRATED PARMESAN
FRESHLY COOKED PASTA (ONE PACKET FOR FOUR PEOPLE)

Sizzle the garlic briefly in the warmed oil, then toss in the broccoli, mixing well, adding salt, pepper, chili and half the parmesan. Mix this with the hot pasta and serve with more parmesan sprinkled on top.

This dish can be made more sophisti-cated by adding a dash of brandy and half a cup of cream to the broccoli mix, warming it really well, and then mixing with the pasta.

Mushroom Pasta Sauce

Life in the House of the Raising Sons spelled chaos and disorder. She who should be obeyed ('Sure, I'll do it just as soon as I've made a few phone calls . . .') had been sorely distracted from the domestic front, leaving the boys to fend for themselves for entire meals.

For some reason, they were unable to execute anything even vaguely resembling a communal dinner. They preferred to do independent kitchen raids in which fanciful improvisational extravaganzas were concocted. Worcestershire sauce and tomato soup, cumin powder and chili were hurled in with salami and eggs and, oh, anything . . . rice bubbles, for all I know.

The result: a ravaged pantry and a fridge full of half-consumed tins and jars of everything from anchovies to baked beans. Onions, too, and tins of sardines. And didn't the fridge smell luscious. Of course, the wastage was appalling. Nobody wants to eat onion-fragrant semi-desiccated sardines, not even the dog. I realised that, no matter how great the life crisis, I was going to have to try to cook ahead or go broke. Short on time and money, I fell back on the good old mushrooms.

1 KG MUSHROOMS, SLICED
BUTTER AS REQUIRED
4 CLOVES GARLIC
SALT TO TASTE
3 TBSPN FINELY CHOPPED
   PARSLEY
1 TSPN DRIED MIXED HERBS
1/2 CUP CREAM

Saute the mushrooms in butter with the garlic and a sprinkling of salt to bring out the juices. When they are softened, add the parsley, herbs and a drizzle of cream. Put the lot through the blender or food processor to transform it to a rough sauce consistency (not soup-like). Spread generously over bowls of freshly cooked pasta with a little grated cheese and sigh with pleasure.

Hear No Evil,
Sea No Evil . . .

If fish is brain food then there's something decidedly on-the-nose about the phrase 'something fishy' having connotations of suspiciousness. 'Something fishy' should be inspirational. But one can only assume it works both ways. I suppose it depends on the bent of brain as to whether the nutritive cerebral stimulus works to the positive or the negative.

Come to think of it, certain teens were up to some extremely fishy secretive boy business after dinner one night. This may not have been mere coincidence. It may have been a direct result of the fish I served them! And if the types of fish are part of the cause and effect, oh dear. What were they up to? I shudder to think. Thank heavens I did not open that door. I had cooked baby shark, which had happened to be the day's bargain special at the market.

Delish Fish Casserole

Interestingly, baby shark was one of the biggest hits ever to be served in the House of the Raising Sons. The household's one and only fish-hater said he'd at last found a fish he loved.

More, more! Of course it was an interesting way to cook fish and suited perfectly the meatiness of young shark, although the recipe works for absolutely any white fish fillets. It is one of those easy, cheap recipes that spruce up a meal into dinner party acceptability.

I am not sure of its origins – it was swapped on the Internet.

3 CUPS FRESH BREADCRUMBS
1½ TBSPN GRATED PARMESAN
1 TSPN FRENCH MUSTARD
1½ TBSPN WORCESTERSHIRE
   SAUCE
½ CUP MELTED BUTTER
1 KG WHITE FISH FILLETS

Mix the crumbs, cheese, mustard, sauce and butter in a large bowl. Place the fish in a lightly greased shallow baking dish and spread the crumb mixture evenly over the top. Cover with greased foil or a lid and bake for about 15 minutes at 180°C until the fish is cooked. Then uncover and bake or grill for a few minutes to brown the top. Serve with salad or vegetables.

Old-fashioned Lemon-baked Fish

If the fishmonger's special is white, boneless fish, then we're home and hosed. One can't go wrong with the happy marriage of these simple, classic ingredients.

1 FISH FILLET PER PERSON
2 TBSPN GOOD OLIVE OIL
2 TBSPN LEMON JUICE
SPRINKLE OF DILL, SALT
   AND PEPPER

Place the fish, well coated and lying in a base of olive oil and lemon, into the oven in an ovenproof dish and bake for about 20 minutes at 200°C (30 minutes for Rudder fish). Season and serve with mashed potato and salad.

Fish and Grape Bake

The busy cook's idea of bliss. Throw it together, put it in the oven, get on with things, and then, voila, a divine dinner!

2 TBSPN OLIVE OIL
1 TBSPN LEMON JUICE
3 TBSPN WHITE WINE
1 TBSPN BUTTER, MELTED
DASH OF WORCESTERSHIRE
   SAUCE
1 FISH FILLET PER PERSON
SALT AND PEPPER TO TASTE
1 CUP HALVED GREEN GRAPES

Combine the oil, lemon, wine, butter and Worcestershire sauce in a casserole dish and roll the fish in the mixture, coating it well. Lie the fish neatly in the dish, lightly salt and pepper and then top with the grapes. Bake in a 200°C oven for 30–40 minutes. Serve with rice and salad or vegetables.

Zesty Baked Fish

A bright and interesting treatment for bland fish.

1 FILLET OF WHITE FISH PER
  PERSON, CUT INTO CHUNKS
2 TBSPN VEGETABLE OIL
2 TBSPN LIGHT SOY SAUCE
2 TBSPN FRESH ORANGE JUICE
1 TBSPN TOMATO SAUCE
1 TSPN LEMON JUICE
1 TBSPN CHOPPED PARSLEY
1 CLOVE GARLIC, CRUSHED
SPRINKLE OF DRIED OREGANO
BLACK PEPPER TO TASTE

Mix all the ingredients in a casserole dish. You can do this in advance to let the fish marinate, although it is not essential. Then cook in a 200°C oven for about half an hour until the fish divides easily when pierced with a knife. Serve with white rice and a vegetable stir-fry.

Kosher Fish Loaf

Okay, it sounds weird. But it is a fun alternative.

1 WHOLE LOAF OF BREAD
1²/₃ CUPS MILK
1 SMALL ONION, FINELY CHOPPED
3 TBSPN BUTTER
750 G CAN AUSSIE SALMON
SALT AND PEPPER TO TASTE

Cut the crusts off the bread and carefully hollow out the inside leaving a 1–2 cm shell. Whiz the insides to fine crumbs and then pour into a saucepan with the milk and stir over low heat until it's like thick, smooth porridge. Add the onion, one tablespoon of butter, the broken-up salmon and seasonings. Mix well and pack into the centre of the loaf. Melt the remaining butter and brush the outside of the loaf. Bake in a 200°C oven until the outside of the bread is a lovely golden brown. This will take only 15 minutes or so. Cool slightly before slicing and serving with salad.

Savoury Flapjacks

Variations on the theme of tinned salmon are many and serve as a good way to ensure the family gets its dose of the precious fish omega oils at the most economical price.

A nifty trick is salmon flapjacks – which are really a sort of savoury drop scone. These work well with cooked side vegetables as a main meal or as a hand-around party snack. And there are no restrictions on the flavourings. The salmon can be replaced with slivered chicken, or, as is preferred by one portion of my boy band, with leftover mixed vegetables for a vegetarian version.

(BASIC RECIPE, WHICH MAKES ABOUT TEN FLAPJACKS)
1/2 CUP BUTTERMILK
1/2 CUP FLOUR
1/4 TSPN BICARB OF SODA
2 EGGS, BEATEN
SALT AND PEPPER TO TASTE

Mix ingredients well into a smooth batter and add either 750 g crumbled salmon or the equivalent of finely diced cooked vegetables. Since they puff out generously, drop only medium-sized spoonfuls into just under 1 cm of very hot vegetable oil in a frying pan, turning once to cook golden brown on both sides. Drain on absorbent paper before serving as finger food or as a main course.

Fishagus Risotto

Fish is brain food. If I had a dollar for every time I told this to boys, I'd be a first-class air traveller. I don't mind them leaning into the vegetarian way of the world. I lean a bit that way, too. But, as a cook responsible for the strength and wellbeing of the next generation, I have bossyboots entitlements – and my nutritional rule for the young vegos was 'fish will be eaten'. Having spread the word, in this era of increasing prices of seafood, one has to spread the rations. This is one of the fish and loaves recipes I devised.

With a pair of tweezers and and some patience, one can make even garfish or snook friendly for bone-phobic eaters. The idea is to find the fish of the day.

2 BUNCHES FRESH ASPARAGUS (ABOUT 400 G – PEAS MAY BE SUBSTITUTED)
400 G BONELESS FISH (YELLOW-EYE MULLET, FLATHEAD OR WHITE-FLESHED FISH)
SALT AND FRESHLY GROUND BLACK PEPPER
2 TBSPN OLIVE OIL
4 SPRING ONIONS, FINELY CHOPPED
500 G ARBORIO RICE
1.5 LITRES HOT VEGETABLE STOCK
1 GLASS WHITE WINE
50 G GRATED PARMESAN
1 TBSPN FINELY CHOPPED FLAT LEAF PARSLEY
1/2 TSPN CHILI POWDER (OPTIONAL)

Cut the asparagus into 2–3 cm pieces, discarding the tough ends, and pre-cook until it is just tender. Remove asparagus and keep the water to add to the stock. Salt and pepper the fish, pan fry it and set it aside. Heat oil in a heavy-based saucepan and soften the spring onions. Add the rice and stir it really well until it glistens with oil then start pouring in the hot stock, including saved vegetable water and wine, stirring and adding a bit at a time. It takes a bit of standing around but, finally, the fluid is absorbed and the consistency in the pot is creamy. Then, throw in the asparagus and the fish, stirring it around until the fish is broken and evenly distributed. Add the parmesan, parsley – and chili, if you wish. Check the seasoning and put the lid on, the heat off and rest the risotto for five or 10 minutes before serving. A cloud of crisp salad at the side is pleasant.

Fresh Salmon on Baby Spinach

On a health binge, I came across a variation on this salady salmon idea. I fell in love with it – and the boys did not argue. It's a summer luxury, and very filling.

600 G ATLANTIC SALMON,
  CAREFULLY DE-BONED AND
  CUT INTO SMALL CUBES
2 TBSPN CANOLA OIL

BLEND:
2 TBSPN SESAME OIL
ZEST OF 1 LARGE NAVEL ORANGE
1/2 CUP ORANGE JUICE
1 TSPN DIJON MUSTARD
1 TBSPN FRESH CHOPPED
  TARRAGON

Fry salmon pieces in canola oil, tossing until they are cooked on all sides. Then add the blended ingredients, raise the heat and toss for 30 seconds.
Remove from heat.

SALAD:
300 G ROUND GREEN BEANS,
  TOPPED AND TAILED AND
  HOT-COOKED
300 G BABY SPINACH OR MIXED
  BABY SALAD GREENS

Arrange salad greens on plates and splay out green beans over the top. Cascade with salmon pieces and drizzle well with the juices.

Kedgeree

How the boys generate such heated discussions on monarchy versus the republic beats me. They bellow around the table of the House of the Raising Sons as if there is an argument. There's not, they're all Aussie republicans.

One week was 'what good did England do to India?' week. And, boy, was England in for a roasting. One of the 'godsons' was raised in India and he had all the facts. Britain inflicted the world's worst banking system on the hapless Indians. It introduced culturally imperialist architecture. It, it, it . . . Biggest boy screamed: 'It raped the land for all it could get!'

'But it built a railway,' ventured a younger one.

'For its own purposes,' hooted biggest. And so the one-sided debate raged. Cricket, golf, linguistic demands, decadence, deluded elitism, profiteering . . .

Hating to admit that I'd ever enjoyed any of the romance of the old Raj tales, I stayed properly mum and kept my message for the next night.

This is it. The one thing I could think of that the British 'gave' to India. Although I suspect it was invented by an Indian cook trying to find something to do with the English passion for smoked fish. It's a wonderful but now little-cooked dish – except at the magnificent Gleneagles Hotel in Scotland, where it is a breakfast fit for kings. Sorry, I mean presidents.

With assorted political grumblings, the boys admitted that Britain's cross-cultural cuisine was a bit of okay. And was there enough for seconds, please?

On this occasion I used local smoked deep-sea bream, because it was cheapest. Cod is the official fish – but any smoked fish should do, since you don't need an awful lot. It's an economical and delicious recipe.

700 G TO 1 KG FLESHY
SMOKED FISH
WATER AS REQUIRED
1/2 LEMON, SLICED
1 BAY LEAF
12 PEPPERCORNS
1–2 STALKS OF PARSLEY
4 SPRING ONIONS, CHOPPED
3 ONIONS, CHOPPED
4 TBSPN BUTTER
1 TBSPN CURRY POWDER
1/2 TSPN CHILI POWDER
31/4 CUPS FISH STOCK
2 CUPS LONG-GRAINED RICE
3–4 HARD-BOILED EGGS,
CHOPPED
3 HEAPED TBSPN CHOPPED
PARSLEY
11/2 TBSPN LEMON JUICE
SALT AND PEPPER TO TASTE

Poach the fish in a pot of water with the lemon, bay leaf, peppercorns, stalks of parsley and one of the chopped spring onions for about 20–30 minutes. Drain the fish, reserving the stock for the rice. Fry the onions in the butter until translucent. Add curry powder and chili and fry for a few more minutes. Add measured and strained stock to the rice in a big pot, tip in the onions, cover and bring to the boil. Reduce to low heat and cook for about 20 minutes, by which time the rice should be tender and the stock absorbed. While the rice is cooking, skin the fish and chop the flesh finely. Add it to the chopped eggs, parsley and remaining spring onions. Add these ingredients to the rice, along with the lemon juice, salt and pepper. Mix everything together well. Cook on a low heat for a few more minutes so the flavours amalgamate. Serve on its own or with a chili relish.

a sensible hat for a person
with only one pair of hands...

Ways to Chicken Out and Serious Bunny Business

....

I chicken out a lot. Every morning I greet my chickens in their corner run of the garden, taking them their daily scraps, refilling their water, casting their wheat and collecting their eggs. They are all called Henrietta. All my chooks over the years have been called Henrietta – except for one. She was called Garbo, because, unlike the thirty-four others I had when I was an organic market gardener in deepest Surrey, England, this chicken wanted to be alone. She left the flock and took up solitary residence in the barn, where I found her one day sitting on a dozen eggs amid the hay bales. This was my cue to use her as a broody on some fertile eggs, which she raised successfully in a broody box in the barn. But once that job was over, she became domesticated and took up residence on the back porch where she nested in one of the dog beds, forcing the hapless dog to sleep on the ground. She also ate the dogs' food, positioning herself between the dogs and fearlessly pecking her share between their wolfing gulps. I never had fresher eggs. She squawked their emergence from just outside the door and I would lean out and collect her warm offering.

Once you have had a life-sharing experience with chickens, there is no going back. I have kept chickens in back yards for twenty years. I cannot imagine life without them and their productive recycling ways.

So it is understandable that I devote a lot of time to honouring them in the kitchen.

Swiss Chicken

How does it come to pass that of all the boys in the House of the Raising Sons, the two brothers have the least in common? It's weird how different siblings can be.

My two are a constant source of irritation to each other. Any sign of brotherly love is veiled in bickering and an endless quest to off-load their chores on to the other. And to challenge for territory. Oh, and how they challenge for territory.

I'd have to sympathise with the older on this issue. He is a settled person with an orderly room and pride in his possessions.

His younger brother, on the other hand, can, within two minutes, spread evidence of his existence to every corner of the house. And he is never happy with his own room. He always wants to be elsewhere but his own bed. There is no settee, couch, bed or even chair in our house in which he has not slept.

Sleeping around the house might be a trifle confusing but it is not nearly as disruptive as room-swapping. And this is his constant ambition. Every move involves a purge. We can't get a foot inside the cellar for his offcasts. He is nothing if not brazen about his decor ambitions. I don't know how many times I've had to explain to him that the living room lounge suite is really more useful for the group if it's in the living room. Surely he doesn't want all of us in his room?

Although that wouldn't worry him a bit. He would doubtlessly be in another room. Probably making another bid on his brother's room – which used to be his room before they swapped about half a dozen swaps ago.

Talk about being as different as chalk and cheese. Which sentiment is most apt for this recipe – being a Swiss dish that has come from America.

The cost of the cheese is offset by the delicious ease of preparation. It is extremely cheesy – but it is also a very kind-to-the-stomach and contenting dish. I serve it on a bed of rice with side-servings of buttered cabbage. But almost any vegetable or salad combination would go as well.

6 CHICKEN BREASTS, HALVED
6 SLICES SWISS CHEESE
1 UNDILUTED CAN CREAM OF
  CHICKEN SOUP
1/4 CUP DRY WHITE WINE
3/4 CUP DRY BREADCRUMBS
1/2 TSPN MIXED DRIED HERBS
1/2 TSPN MEDIUM CHILI POWDER
A LITTLE MELTED BUTTER

Arrange the chicken in a greased casserole and top with cheese slices. Combine the soup and wine and pour over. Sprinkle with breadcrumbs, herbs and chili, pour over butter and bake in a 180°C oven for 45–55 minutes.

Chicken in Currant Sauce

A fast meal which fools them every time. It tastes as if it involved some effort.

SKINNED CHICKEN BREASTS –
  ABOUT ONE PER PERSON

SAUCE:
1 JAR REDCURRANT
  (OR CRANBERRY) JELLY
2 TBSPN WORCESTERSHIRE
  SAUCE
3 TBSPN LEMON JUICE
SALT AND BLACK PEPPER
  TO TASTE
2 TSPN MIXED SPICE
1/2 TSPN CHILI POWDER
1 TBSPN CORNFLOUR
1 CUP WATER

Mix the sauce ingredients in a saucepan and heat, stirring, until it thickens. Simmer a few minutes to cook through. Slice the chicken meat into long strips and place in an open baking dish, pouring the sauce over the top. Bake at about 200°C for 40 minutes. Serve with mashed potato or steamed rice and some hearty buttered vegetables.

Chicken Potroast

We were watching one of those typical American family movies one night when my older son snapped. 'I can't take it any longer!' he screamed. 'What in heaven's name is a potroast?'

Funnily enough, I'd been wondering the same thing for years. Americans always seem to be planning to have 'potroasts' in their movies. Yet we never see them do it.

The 'potroast' must be the last American mystery. But in the House of the Raising Sons, it's a mystery no longer.

Debate raged at the dinner table after I had unearthed the secrets of the dish and finally cooked it à la chicken. It's a quaint sort of a roast. One of the boys described it as a 'wet roast'. It certainly is homely, and it is definitely nutritious, filling and economical.

In essence, chicken potroast is a plain dish. It would be very easy to pep it up with herbs, chili, a dash of Worcestershire sauce or a flavoursome bacon or olive-enriched stuffing. Then again, the vegetable and chicken flavours do harmonise well and not every meal needs to be exotic.

1 LARGE ROASTING CHICKEN
6 SMALL ONIONS OR 3 LARGE
  ONES, HALVED
5 MEDIUM POTATOES, HALVED
4 CARROTS, ROUGHLY CHOPPED
1 CUP STOCK
1 CUP PEAS
1 CUP SLICED MUSHROOMS
1 CUP OTHER VEGETABLES
SALT TO TASTE

BREAD STUFFING:
ANY STANDARD BREAD STUFFING
WILL DO. I USE 3 CUPS LIGHT
WHOLEMEAL CRUMBS,
1/2 GRATED ONION,
2 TBSPN CHOPPED PARSLEY,
2 TSPN CHOPPED FRESH LOVAGE
AND THYME, 1/2 COOKED QUINCE
DICED FINELY, 1 EGG, SALT, LOTS
OF FRESH BLACK PEPPER AND
WATER TO BIND.

Remove the parson's nose, stuff the chook and tie up its legs. Place in a large casserole and put, uncovered, into a hot 220°C oven for 15 minutes. Add the onions, cover and bake for 30 minutes, lowering the heat to about 190°C after 15 minutes. Then add potatoes, carrots and the stock. Cover again and cook for 30 minutes. Add the other vegetables and salt and return to the oven for another 30 minutes.

Garlic Potroast

Feed a cold? Surely the idea is to feed against a cold. I hate colds and I'm not too keen on people with colds. That's why the House of the Raising Sons, which always relies on seasonal foods, specialises in anti-colds fare in winter.

One can't always ward off colds where boys are concerned. Apart from their habit of socialising with huge packs of their peers in closely confined spaces, they catch colds by losing money. Well, by their perpetual ineptitude at budgeting which means that they end up marching home in the rain because, oops, they hadn't kept enough money for a fare. I throw up my arms in despair.

The counterplot is preventive tucker. This particular gem, which the boys relish with unmitigated greed, has the added bonus of keeping them at a reasonable distance from the contagions of society. They end up arms-length aromatic.

This is absolutely not the recipe for garlic-shy people. They can get their colds and keep them, if you ask me. Good old garlic is nature's magic medicine. Folklore reckons it cures everything from athlete's foot and ringworm to cancer and cholera. I wouldn't go that far. But I do believe it helps boost the immune system and fights bacteria. It's also supposed to lower cholesterol and combat heart disease and strokes. For proper benefit, it should be eaten raw. However, in this instance, we like it cooked and in plenty.

Warning. This is a messy meal. It should be consumed with good, fresh bread to soak up the juices. Fingers are used to tackle the garlic, so finger bowls are a must. But it's a very clean dish to cook and incredibly cheap and easy. I'd describe it as a French sort of potroast.

40 CLOVES GARLIC, UNPEELED
1/2 CUP OLIVE OIL
1 LARGE CHICKEN
FRESH HERBS AS REQUIRED
SALT AND PEPPER TO TASTE

Spread the unpeeled garlic cloves over the bottom of a casserole or ovenproof pot, pour over half the oil, put the chicken on top, pack lots of fresh assorted herbs (thyme, sage, marjoram, parsley, bay leaves – but not tarragon) around the outside of the chicken, pour the rest of the olive oil over the top, sprinkle with salt and pepper. Cover closely and bake in the middle of a 180–200°C oven for about one-and-a-half hours. Serve chicken with sauce and lots of cloves of garlic, which you either slop out onto fresh bread or suck out of the skins as you go. Messy but marvellous!

Honey Chicken Marinade

Anticipation of vegetarian vacation is a criminal act. My vego zealot went into a paranoid lather of 'boy, you really want me out of here' just because he came across some chicken wings in the bottom of the fridge innocently marinating in the world's best honey chicken sauce. After much hugging and reassurance, we managed to convince him that we love him dearly – but we love honey chicken, too.

4 TBSPN RUNNY HONEY
2 TBSPN SOY SAUCE
2 TSPN GRATED FRESH GINGER
2 TBSPN DRY SHERRY
2 TSPN FIVE SPICE POWDER
1/2 TSPN SESAME OIL
1 1/2 KG CHICKEN WINGS

Blend ingredients in a large bowl and add chicken wings, coating carefully. Cover with cling film and store for a day or so in the bottom of the fridge rotating the wings occasionally in the bowl to ensure they all get a good share of the marinade. When ready to eat, place the wings and sauce in a large baking tray and bake in a 180°C oven for 50 minutes, turning once half-way through to ensure the wings are golden brown on both sides. Serve with a drizzle of the sauce on some plain steamed rice. Garnish with lots of sliced cucumber.

Chicken Noodle Casserole

Here's a classic poverty tucker recipe, which is one of those wonderfully versatile gems that can be adapted to all manner of vegetables and flavourings. Your imagination is the only limitation. The basic idea is chicken and noodles. Tomatoes, blanched broccoli florets, blanched pumpkin slivers, even bean sprouts are a goer in lieu of the vegies suggested. All measurements are variable. The big trick is that the whole thing makes a little chicken go a long and yummy way.

1 CUP DRY BREADCRUMBS
1 MEDIUM ONION,
   FINELY CHOPPED
SALT AND GROUND BLACK
   PEPPER TO TASTE
1 TSPN CHILI POWDER
1 TBSPN FINELY CHOPPED
   PARSLEY
4 CUPS COOKED NOODLES
   (OR MORE)
250 G SLICED MUSHROOMS
1/2 BUNCH SPINACH LEAVES,
   CHOPPED
2 CUPS DICED COOKED CHICKEN
1 CUP GRATED CHEDDAR CHEESE
   OR 1/2 CUP PARMESAN
2 CUPS HOT CHICKEN STOCK

Make a loose mixture of the breadcrumbs, onion, salt, pepper, chili and parsley. Put a layer of noodles in a large, well-greased casserole. Sprinkle lightly with the crumble seasonings, then layer mushrooms, spinach and chicken, also sprinkled with the seasoning mix. Spread the cheese on top of the chicken and cover with the rest of the noodles, allowing a goodly last sprinkling of the seasonings on top. Pour on the chicken stock and bake, uncovered, in a 180°C oven for 30–40 minutes, after which time the top should be golden brown. Serve with a tomato or green salad.

Poached Chicken

There are lots of ways of having cold chicken but when the associated advantages are counted out in this context, I far prefer to use chicken that has been poached rather than roasted.

There are also lots of ways to poach a chicken. Using onions spiked with cloves, carrots and peppercorns is the usual western style which produces a very pleasant stock to keep in the fridge for use in soups, sauces and general flavouring.

I rarely choose this option. The gentle piquance of both stock and flesh produced by Asian-style chicken poaching has an edge over the old, familiar style – and what is produced at the end of these recipes is a cheap yet elegant cross-cultural meal which will fit into the busiest of lifestyles. First the chicken:

1 LARGE CHOOK
ALL YOUR STAINLESS STEEL
   SPOONS
COLD WATER AS REQUIRED
ABOUT 6 CM FRESH ROOT GINGER
3–4 SPRING ONIONS
ABOUT 8 PEPPERCORNS

If the bird is large and fleshy and you wish to keep it delicate, moist and tender by not overcooking it, the trick is, after washing and cutting off the parson's nose and any extra fat, to pack the body cavity with stainless steel spoons. I ram in most of the household supply. It's an odd way to stuff a chicken and guaranteed to raise laughs of incredulity from witnesses, but the heat accumulated in the metal helps to cook the bird thoroughly from within.

So, stuff the bird with spoons, cover three-quarters of it with cold water, add the roughly chopped ginger and spring onions along with the peppercorns, and bring the pot, covered, to the boil. Give it five minutes' boiling, turn down to simmer for 20 minutes, and then turn off the heat and, leaving the bird covered, let it continue to cook as it cools in the stock. When it is cold, either drain the bird and strain the stock to store in the fridge, or put the whole pot in the fridge to keep cold and fresh for the next night's dinner.

Sauce Veronique

So that cold chicken becomes more than the straight salad and mayo, sandwich or rehash options but is nevertheless a high-class and economical meal, serve it with Veronique sauce. It's simply magic and also probably the easiest sauce ever to come out of France.

2 EGG YOLKS
1 CUP CREAM
1 SMALL GLASS DRY SHERRY
2 TSPN GRATED LEMON PEEL

Beat the egg yolks into the cream with the sherry and stir the mixture over a low heat until it has thickened slightly. It is a light sauce so it will not thicken like a white sauce. It will be quite runny but thick enough, when cooled, to coat chicken appetisingly. After cooking, cool the sauce in the fridge and then pour over poached chicken pieces, sprinkling generously with finely grated lemon peel. This is pleasant served with warm mashed potatoes or assorted side salads.

House of the Raising Sons Roast Chook

For a real blow-out dinner, our idea of a big treat is a large free-range chook bulked out with a spectacular stuffing. To make the bird stretch to feed eight people, you should not exclude any of the trimmings. I'm not about to tell you exactly how to roast a chook. Mrs Beeton will do that for any new cook. These chook tips are for turning roast chicken into a major luxury meal.

1 LARGE CHOOK
OIL AS REQUIRED
4–6 RASHERS OF BACON
VEGETABLES AS REQUIRED

STUFFING:
1 MEDIUM ONION, GRATED
200–250 G KALAMATA OLIVES,
    STONED AND FINELY SLICED
1–1½ CUPS DRIED
    BREADCRUMBS
1 EGG
1 TSPN VINEGAR
2–3 TBSPN CHOPPED PARSLEY
SALT AND PEPPER TO TASTE
A DRIZZLE OF HOT WATER

GRAVY:
2 TBSPN FLOUR
½ CUP WINE (RED OR WHITE)
WATER AS REQUIRED
DASH OF WORCESTERSHIRE
    SAUCE
DASH OF MUSHROOM SOY SAUCE
1 TBSPN REDCURRENT JELLY OR
    CRANBERRY SAUCE
SALT AND PEPPER TO TASTE

Mix all stuffing ingredients together thoroughly, adding enough water to get a soft, mouldable consistency, then stuff the bird's body cavity and also under the skin from the neck. Gently ease the skin away from the flesh with the hand and make a pocket large enough to fill with half the stuffing. Lightly oil the roasting pan and the bird. Cover the top of the bird generously with rashers of bacon and, for the first hour, a loose piece of foil. Roast in the usual way along with lashings of assorted vegetables. When resting the cooked bird, make up the gravy in the baking pan, pouring off excess fat but leaving enough fat and juices to make a roux. After mixing in flour, add wine and slowly stir in water (I use the vegetable water left from whatever vegies I've steamed), Worcestershire and soy sauce, jelly and seasoning.

Southern Fried Chicken

This is the way they traditionally do it in the United States and I have never found anyone who didn't love it.

1 CUP PLAIN FLOUR
SALT AND BLACK PEPPER
   TO TASTE
1 TSPN PAPRIKA
2 EGGS, BEATEN WITH 1 CUP
   OF MILK
1 CUP VEGETABLE OIL
4–5 CHICKEN PORTIONS

Mix the flour, pepper, salt and paprika together in one bowl and the beaten egg and milk in another. Keep them close to a frying pan in which the oil is medium-hot. Dip the prepared joints of chicken first in the egg and then in the flour before popping them in the pan to fry to a crispy, golden brown on both sides. Serve with mashed potatoes and Fried Green Tomatoes (see recipe page 127).

Chicken California

Another American Internet goodie which is so sublime it even impresses at dinner parties.

6 SKINLESS CHICKEN BREAST
   FILLETS
3/4 CUP SOY SAUCE (LIGHT
   IS OKAY)
1/4 CUP BROWN SUGAR
1 TBSPN VEGETABLE OIL
2 TBSPN VINEGAR
1 LARGE CLOVE GARLIC, CRUSHED
1 MEDIUM ONION, SLICED
4–5 YELLOW PEACHES,
   PEELED AND SLICED

Score the chicken and place in a bowl with a well-mixed marinade consisting of all the remaining ingredients except the peaches. Refrigerate for an hour or so, turning the chicken once or twice. Remove the chicken and cook under a hot grill or on a pan in the oven until it is cooked through. Meanwhile, simmer the leftover marinade until the onion is tender and, just before serving, add the peach slices. Serve the sauce poured over the chicken on a bed of white rice.

Save the Reputation Chicken

So named when I let dinner burn in the oven and had to come up with something quick and tasty – or face a rebellious starving mass. This is a favourite Kangaroo Island recipe, in honour of the island's famous Ligurian bees.

1½ KG CHICKEN PIECES
3 TBSPN BUTTER

SAUCE:
1 CUP HONEY (A GOOD WAY TO GET RID OF AGEING CANDIED HONEY)
1 CUP LEMON JUICE
2 TSPN GROUND GINGER
1 CUP WATER

Divide the chicken pieces at the joint, trimming off excess skin and fat, and brown well on both sides in butter in a large frypan. Meanwhile, warm the sauce ingredients until the honey is runny (you can microwave them) and then pour over the browned chicken pieces, reducing the heat to low before covering and allowing to simmer gently for about an hour. Serve with white rice and some undressed lettuce or green sprouts on the side.

Rotopoulo Metaxa (Brandied Chicken)

It's also possible to use cheap chicken pieces for quite posh dinners. The ingredients have to be a bit more up-market but if you keep the old medicinal brandy in the house, this version of an old Greek recipe is a rewarding use for it. It stood me in good stead way back when, as a young doctor's wife, I tremulously turned on formal dinners for the big-time consultants or professors.

1 YOUNG CHICKEN, JOINTED
JUICE OF HALF A LEMON
1/4 CUP BUTTER
1/4 CUP BRANDY
1/4 CUP THICK CREAM
SALT AND PEPPER

Toss the chicken in the lemon, season with salt and pepper. Meanwhile, heat the butter in a heavy-based saucepan. Carefully cook the chicken, turning regularly until it is golden brown on all sides and pretty well cooked through. Add the brandy and simmer, turning the chicken, until the brandy is absorbed. Then pour on the cream and heat through but do not boil. Check seasoning and serve with mashed potatoes or ribbon noodles.

Chicken with Olives

Since there are so many of us meandering around the House of the Raising Sons, we tend not to eat out much. It would be exorbitant. And, quite frankly, more often than not when I eat out, I wish I'd eaten at home.

Eating out can be so disappointing. The biggest thrill is often the menu with all its salivatory promise. The imagination runs riot and choosing can be the hardest part of the meal.

Then there's the waiting. I often wonder why they call the table attendants waiters since they are the busy ones. It's the patrons who do the waiting. A lot of waiting sometimes.

There's the sipping of drinks, the art of animated small talk, the picking at breadrolls and the waiting and the waiting. Perhaps the idea is that the longer you wait the more hungry you become, and the more hungry you become the less critical you are about what you eat – because often the food turns out to be not nearly as interesting as it seemed in concept on the menu.

With that philosophy in mind, eating at home is quite a treat. This is a dish I wished had been cooked my way when I made the mistake of ordering it at a restaurant. It's a homely old European classic which goes well with rice or mashed potatoes. If you shred the chicken, it goes very nicely with pasta, too.

she pressed on against the odds ...

3 ONIONS, CHOPPED
3 CLOVES GARLIC, CRUSHED
6 TSPN OLIVE OIL
1 TSPN DRIED MIXED HERBS
1 TBSPN CHOPPED PARSLEY
1 KG SKINLESS CHICKEN
   BREASTS
SALT AND FRESHLY GROUND
   BLACK PEPPER TO TASTE
1 LARGE TIN TOMATOES,
   CRUSHED
1/2 CUP WHITE WINE
1/2 TSPN CHILI POWDER
1 CUP CHOPPED BLACK OLIVES
SQUEEZE OF LEMON JUICE

Fry the onions and garlic in half the oil until they start to caramelise. Mix in the herbs. Meanwhile, slice and season the chicken and gently brown in the rest of the oil. Pour in the tomatoes and wine and simmer until the liquid begins to reduce. Add the onions, chili, olives and lemon juice. Cook a little longer to amalgamate the flavours before serving.

Mushrooms with Chicken

Stir-frys have become so ubiquitous, I have come to hate the name. But you can't beat a light and healthy stir-fry quickie after a hard day in the office.

SALT TO TASTE
2 TSPN BRANDY
2 TSPN SOY SAUCE
2 TSPN GRATED GINGER
2 TSPN CORNFLOUR
OIL AS REQUIRED
3 CHICKEN BREASTS, DICED
2 CLOVES GARLIC, CRUSHED
350 G MUSHROOMS, SLICED
1 TBSPN OYSTER SAUCE
1^1/5 CUPS WATER

In a bowl add the salt, brandy, soy sauce, ginger, cornflour and a little drizzle of oil to the chicken and mix well together. In a hot, oiled frying pan, sizzle the garlic until it's beginning to brown. Then pour in the chicken and stir-fry until semi-cooked. Add mushrooms and oyster sauce, stirring. Pour on the water. Continue to stir until the chicken is thoroughly cooked and the sauce is rich and thick. Serve sprinkled with spring onions on hot white rice.

Royal Chicken

Multiculturalism is passé. Zapping along the information superhighway, we have arrived in the global village – and I am right at home. I think everybody should be there. I think people without email are akin to troglodytes. How do they function?

The boys of the House of the Raising Sons set me free onto the Internet when they were but puppies. They turned me into an 'early adopter' – and, among other dividends, they scored a whole new world of international taste sensations. Food is one of those exquisite commonalities that bond us all, even via fibre optic cables.

I quickly became one of those who can work all day on one computer and then play all night on another – blogging, chatting, Twittering, pinging links on StumbleUpon, making Scrabble moves, uploading Flickr photos and generally dancing around the morass of what has come to be known as social media.

I was born for it.

The boys love computer connectivity and are whizzy with the technology – but they remain somewhat gobsmacked at what they unleashed in Mum. She takes her laptop to bed with her, for heaven's sake. Too much information is never enough. Insufficient sleep is too much.

I now have circles and spirals and, oh, yes, I admit it, networks of friends, people all around the borderless world who share interests, values and humour. We not only write and talk but we travel and climb comfortably under the skins of each other's cultures. Hence I now have homes-away-from-home in the USA. I not only have the wealth of new recipes, but I have even tested them in foreign kitchens.

This recipe comes from Las Cruces in New Mexico and I first cooked it in New Hampshire.

1 TBSPN BUTTER
2 LARGE ONIONS, CHOPPED
1¹/₂ CUPS MUSHROOMS, SLICED
1¹/₂ KG CHICKEN PIECES
1 CUP HOT WATER
SALT AND PEPPER TO TASTE
1 TBSPN PLAIN FLOUR
2 TSPN PAPRIKA
1 CUP SOUR CREAM

Fry together in the butter the onions, mushrooms and chicken until the chicken is golden, then add water, salt and pepper, cover and simmer until the chicken is tender. Blend the flour with paprika and sour cream, stir carefully into the sauce and cook until the sauce is thickened. Serve with mashed potatoes or ribbon noodles.

Peaceful Summer Stew

One of those dishes you can cook in phases while doing other things – a summer Sunday evening sort of thing.

OIL AS REQUIRED
1 MEDIUM ONION, CHOPPED
1 PLUMP CLOVE GARLIC,
   CRUSHED
2 WAXY POTATOES, DICED
1 LARGE CARROT, THINLY SLICED
1 LARGE RIPE TOMATO, CHOPPED
2 RED CAPSICUMS, DICED
1 GREEN CAPSICUM, DICED
4 ZUCCHINIS, SLICED
SALT AND FRESHLY GROUND
   BLACK PEPPER TO TASTE
2 GREEN CHILIES
¹/₂ KG CHICKEN BREASTS,
   THINLY DICED
1 BUNCH FRESH BASIL
¹/₂ TSPN DRIED THYME
2 CUPS WATER
1 VEGETABLE STOCK CUBE

Heat the oil and add onion and garlic. Saute briefly and add the potato, carrot, tomato and capsicums. Stir well and simmer, stirring occasionally. When the vegetables begin to soften add sliced zucchinis and salt, and continue as before. Toss in chopped chilies and chicken. When the chicken is almost cooked, roughly chop the basil and add it, along with thyme, salt and pepper. Simmer a little longer and then add the water and stock cube. Keep simmering until the chicken is well cooked and a fragrant, light sauce has developed. Serve with ribbon egg noodles.

Quinces and Chicken

My quince supplier's tip is to bake fresh quinces slowly for six hours in a low oven. The result is a stock that can be refrigerated and is ready to add to cakes or other dishes. For this dish I peeled, quartered and slowly stewed the quinces in a little water so I could use the syrup.

2 MEDIUM ONIONS, CHOPPED
3 TBSPN BUTTER AND OIL MIXED
1/2 KG CHICKEN THIGH FILLETS
SEASONED PLAIN FLOUR
    FOR COATING
1 LARGE TOMATO
4–5 COOKED QUINCES
1 TBSPN CURRY POWDER
2 TSPN CHOPPED FRESH BASIL
    OR 1 TSPN DRIED BASIL
SALT AND LOTS OF FRESHLY
    GROUND BLACK PEPPER
    TO TASTE
AT LEAST 1 TBSPN SUGAR

Soften the onions in the butter and oil. Toss the chicken fillets in the seasoned flour and fry on both sides with the onion. Chop and add the tomato, then the cooked quinces in medium-sized portions and some of their cooking juices, the curry powder and herbs. Stew this on a medium heat until the quinces begin to disintegrate. Add salt and pepper and then sugar to your own taste – at least one tablespoon is needed unless you like your food very tart. Serve with steamed white rice and, for the aesthetics and nutritional balance of things, a green vegetable of some sort.

Chicken and Quince Stew

This is a version of Tagine, the famous Moroccan dish. The Moroccans know how well quinces complement meats.

2 TBSPN BUTTER
1½ KG CHEAP CHICKEN PIECES
3 ONIONS, FINELY CHOPPED
WATER AS REQUIRED
SALT AND PEPPER TO TASTE
1 TSPN GROUND GINGER
1 TSPN TURMERIC
1 TSPN PAPRIKA
1 BUNCH FRESH PARSLEY,
  CHOPPED
1 KG QUINCES

In a large, heavy-based saucepan, melt butter and fry the jointed chicken pieces and onion until the chicken is whitish and the onion becomes translucent. Then add enough water to almost cover the chicken, but not to swamp it. Season with salt, lots of freshly ground black pepper, ginger, turmeric, paprika and parsley. You can add a pinch of chili if you want to. Bring to the boil and them simmer gently for a good hour. Meanwhile, wash and rub the down from the skin of the quinces but do not peel them. Slice the fruit into quarters and core, as with apples. Pop the fruit in with the chicken and cook for a further 20 minutes or until the quinces are tender. Then serve with rice to absorb the juices. If you find the quinces too tart, add one teaspoon of sugar to the juice before serving.

Chicken Hush

As we age, we get invisible wrinkles as well as the ones so obvious to the world. I have discovered that the invisible wrinkles are even harder to hide.

I can't help showing my age when the lads are having band practice in the House of the Raising Sons. It's not that their music is not good. It's terrific. I am sure the neighbours about four blocks away think it is very pretty. The lads have worked with immense discipline and professionalism and their harmonies are marvellous. But the volume?

As they stand there, mikes in hand, singing amid their amplifiers and a battery of electrical equipment, I don't even pause to worry about their potential hearing loss. I simply run for cover behind as many doors as I can close. My spirit is young but my inner ears have aged. Clearly they have developed a mass of tiny, tender auditory wrinkles. And they can't cope with cacophony.

They suffer in all those trendy restaurants which have been redesigned under the sad assumption that people can't be having a good time unless they can't hear themselves think. The tummy may be rewarded by good food but the ears are punished by unnecessary pounding.

Hiding from the youthful barrage of beat, it was in pondering this association of food and aural suffering that I had the brainwave – seduce the lads from their clamorous creativity with their favourite thing, food.

And thus did this mum still the ringing in her long-assaulted ears and bring peace upon the house. She played chicken – and won.

The loud approbation of the boys, who were still in shout mode, was music to her ears. This American domestic dish tastes terrific.

600 G CHICKEN BREAST MEAT,
SLICED INTO BROAD STRIPS
1/3 CUP MAYONNAISE
3/4 CUP BREADCRUMBS
SALT AND PEPPER TO TASTE

SAUCE:
1 CUP MAYONNAISE
1/2 CUP MILK
1/2 CUP GRATED CHEDDAR CHEESE
1 TBSPN GRATED PARMESAN
1 TSPN DRIED THYME LEAVES

Toss the chicken in the mayonnaise. Season breadcrumbs and coat chicken pieces. Place in a greased baking pan and bake in a 180°C oven for about 35 minutes (turning once for even brownness). Meanwhile, combine the sauce ingredients and cook over a medium heat, stirring, for about 10 minutes. Serve poured over the chicken pieces, accompanied either by potatoes with vegetables or rice and salad.

Sly Slimmer's Paprika Chicken

If I'm on a diet, everyone is on a diet. That is the cook's power. Of course it is better to say nothing or boys are watching to see if weight is lost and, worse, they are protesting that they, as sedentary sports heroes, need all the calories they can get.

This is a sensationally low-fat dish but so substantial and delicious that no one would ever imagine it is diet food, especially if you serve it to them with lashings of buttered ribbon egg noodles and a pile of green beans.

1 YELLOW ONION, FINELY CHOPPED
2 TBSPN HUNGARIAN PAPRIKA
(SWEET PAPRIKA)
1/2 TSPN CHILI POWDER (OPTIONAL)
4 SKINLESS CHICKEN BREASTS,
CUBED
2 KG RIPE TOMATOES, PEELED AND
CHOPPED
1/2 CUP CHICKEN BROTH
SALT AND PEPPER
LOW-FAT SOUR CREAM

Soften onion in oil in a large pan before stirring in the paprika and chili powder. Integrate well and add the chicken. Stir over a medium heat until the flesh is white on all sides and then add tomatoes and chicken broth. Stir well, cover and simmer for 30 minutes. Season and serve over ribbon egg noodles or rice with a dollop of sour cream.

Down-under Jambalaya

The joy of Internet communications is the human elucidation you can get on little things that puzzle you. I had wondered about jambalaya since hearing a pop song about having jambalaya and cat fish pie when I was a girl. An American Southerner net friend was happy to explain that it's nothing more than a rice stew. She described the recipe and I adapted it to what we had to hand. It was delicious.

1 KG CHICKEN PIECES
WATER AS REQUIRED
5 CM FRESH GINGER, SLICED
3 ONIONS
2 CUPS JASMINE RICE
1 TSPN TURMERIC
SALT AND FRESHLY GROUND
   BLACK PEPPER TO TASTE
2 CAPSICUMS
1 TBSPN OLIVE OIL
$1/2$ TBSPN BUTTER
2 SMALL CANS PEELED
   TOMATOES, CHOPPED
2 GREEN CHILIES, SLICED
3 TBSPN CHOPPED PARSLEY

Trim and just cover the chicken pieces with water in a heavy-based pot. Add the ginger and one peeled onion and simmer until the chicken is tender. Strain the stock. Place the rice in a heavy-based saucepan with a secure lid. Add three cups of the stock, a teaspoon of turmeric and a dash of salt. Bring to the boil, turn off and leave for 30 minutes. Meanwhile, chop the other two onions and capsicum and saute steadily in the oil and butter until the onions are translucent and the capsicums tender. Strip the chicken meat from the bone. Add chicken and chopped tomatoes to the vegetables along with the chilies and parsley. Cook together for a while to amalgamate the flavours. Finally, tease out the rice with a fork and add it to the mixed meat and vegetables with pepper and salt to taste. Toss everything together and serve piping hot with a salad.

This recipe can be adapted for vegetarians. Cook the rice in vegetable stock or with a vegetable stock cube, a couple of slices of ginger (to be removed when cooked) and turmeric. Add peas, grated carrot and mushrooms to the cooked vegetable mixture in lieu of the chicken.

One of the world's loneliest jobs.

Scone-topped Chicken

News on the food budget front is often grim. Meat prices to rise. Threats of deregulation price increases. Wheat crops disrupted and possible bread price hikes. As the shoestring gets shorter, culinary imagination has to expand.

They're not going to beat us. Our grandmothers survived the Depression. Families coped on rations. Even now in Eastern Europe and even parts of South America, mums are inventing sustaining meals from meagre supplies. We really have nothing to grumble about. Australia is still a land of plenty. We just have to adjust our diets to include more seasonal fruits and vegies, and use age-old techniques to stretch luxuries.

By glorious chance, I happened upon a fantastic meal-stretcher dish. Its sumptuous moreishness belies its economy – and it's so filling that orders greedily put in for seconds when my rapacious boys had just begun to eat were reluctantly cancelled as they finished their serves. Instead, they asked if I wouldn't mind cooking the whole thing again the next night.

I found this recipe in one of those odd old recipe books printed on cheap paper. I'd credit its creator, except that there are no attributions in the book. Sad. Whoever invented this obviously very English dish deserves a big hug.

STEP ONE: THE CHICKEN

2 TBSPN BUTTER
2 TBSPN PLAIN FLOUR
2¹/₂ CUPS CHICKEN STOCK
APPROX 500 G COOKED
 CHICKEN MEAT
SALT AND BLACK PEPPER
 TO TASTE
3 TBSPN CREAM
3 TBSPN DRY SHERRY
4 TBSPN PARMESAN

Melt butter, add flour and stir for a minute before drizzling in the chicken stock and stirring until it thickens. Then toss in the chicken, salt, pepper, cream and sherry. Mix well and turn into a broad casserole dish. Sprinkle the parmesan on top.

STEP TWO: THE SCONES

2 CUPS SELF-RAISING FLOUR
SALT AND BLACK PEPPER
   TO TASTE
2 TBSPN DRY MUSTARD
90 G BUTTER
2 EGGS, BEATEN
3 TBSPN CREAM

Place dry ingredients in a large bowl and rub in butter with your finger tips until the mix is crumblyish. Mix the eggs with the cream. Make a well in the middle of the flour and pour in the eggs, stirring until all the flour is absorbed and you have a good, firm dough. Knead on a board, then roll to about 5 mm thickness and cut into scone-sized rounds. Arrange these on top of the chicken, brush with a little milk and bake, open, in a 250°C oven for 15–20 minutes.

every dog...
has its day.

Regular Chicken

They told me they didn't like prunes, especially stewed prunes. Yuk!

With two decades of motherhood under my belt, I took no notice. Boys, even big adult boys, have a nasty habit of saying they don't like things without ever having tried them.

I've deviously had my mob eating things for yonks that they supposedly hate. Why should prunes be different? I love them and they're madly healthy. Apart from their famous fibre, they're full of iron, potassium and precious carotene. Nourish the boys until they scream for mercy, I say.

Which is how it came to pass that every last one of my coterie of lanky lads, except the vego, was eating prunes with effusive relish. The only sounds they made were sensual murmurs of pleasure until they asked for seconds. And seconds is a modest description for the way they cleared the pan. The silly thing is they still think they hate stewed prunes – yet what they'd devoured to the last lick was just that, stewed prunes with chicken.

4 LARGE ONIONS, CHOPPED
2 TBSPN OIL
1–1½ KG CHICKEN PIECES
WATER AS REQUIRED
500 G PRUNES
SALT AND PEPPER TO TASTE

Fry the onions in the oil in a large pan until they're soft and translucent. Place the jointed chicken portions on the onion, almost submerge in about one-and-a-half cups of water, cover the pan and simmer on medium heat for about 45 minutes. Pit the prunes and add to the pan. Cover and cook for 20 minutes then take the lid off and stir the prunes well so they amalgamate and turn the juices into a thick sauce. Simmer another 10–15 minutes until the chicken is tender and the sauce is rich and gravy-like. Season and serve with steamed rice and a green side salad.

Marmalade Chicken

Turning back the clock doesn't stop one from having to chase it. Life seems to run into more of a rush as the years roll on.

That was the only excuse I could give when I realised that in my speed trolley-push down the supermarket aisles, I had overlooked a few essential grocery items. I had remembered to buy chicken and rice and salad vegies and milk and cereal and dogfood and washing powder ... but a few other useful items had been rushed past. And come cooking time, I was in a jam.

And so I came to use, well, not so much jam, as marmalade, in a chicken recipe. Once again, the inspiration was from America. Once again it was gleaned, indirectly, from the never-ending resources of the Internet.

I would never have thought off my own bat to spoon the morning marmalade into the chicken. But I think I will be doing it more often after this hasty dish, which was enjoyed by even the fussier eaters in the House of the Raising Sons.

1 CUP SLICED ALMONDS
4 TBSPN BUTTER
CHICKEN BREASTS (ONE PER PERSON – THIS QUANTITY OF SAUCE IS ENOUGH FOR SIX FILLETS)
SALT AND BLACK PEPPER TO TASTE
2 TBSPN MARMALADE
4 TSPN FRENCH MUSTARD
1 CUP CREAM
DASH OF CAYENNE PEPPER

Saute the almonds in butter to light brown and reserve. Flatten and slice the chicken breasts, season and lightly fry for a few minutes. Add the rest of the ingredients and simmer until sauce thickens. Serve with steamed white rice, stirring the almonds into the sauce at the last moment.

Ginger Chicken and Pineapple Salad

This fresh and healthy dish makes for lovely summer evening fare.

1 PINEAPPLE
1 LARGE COOKED CHICKEN
ABOUT 3 CM FRESH GINGER,
    GRATED
1 SMALL ONION, SLICED
1 RED CAPSICUM, FINELY SLICED
1/4 CUP CHOPPED PARSLEY
1/4 CUP GRAPES, HALVED
HERBED FRENCH DRESSING
    AS REQUIRED
SALT AND FRESHLY GROUND
    BLACK PEPPER TO TASTE

For presentation, the pineapple can be halved lengthwise with the flesh cut out so the shells can be used as serving containers. Otherwise, cut the pineapple and cube the flesh. Bone the chicken and cube the meat. Combine the ginger, onion, capsicum, parsley and grapes and stir thoroughly into the chicken. Add dressing and toss. Season and serve chilled.

she was out-standing-in-her-field ...

Tangelo Chicken

Tangelos have the best rinds in the citrus business. They are also extremely juicy. And they have a piquance somewhere between an orange and a mandarin, which makes them better than either for a tangy, citrusy dish. This is a truly elegant yet easy meal.

2 TBSPN MARGARINE
8 CHICKEN THIGH FILLETS
5 TANGELOS
2 TSPN CASTER SUGAR
1/2 TSPN PAPRIKA
1/4 TSPN CAYENNE
SALT TO TASTE
SLIVERED ALMONDS
  AS REQUIRED

Melt margarine in a frypan and fry chicken fillets thoroughly on both sides. While they are cooking, lightly grate just the outer rind from four of the tangelos and juice them. Peel the fifth one and chop it up roughly. Pour off excess margarine from the frying pan and add the tangelo juice, rind and pieces along with the sugar and seasonings. Allow this to simmer away until the sauce is reduced and thickening. Meanwhile, in a small lightly oiled frying pan, brown some slivered almonds. Serve the chicken with the sauce spooned on top and a sprinkling of almonds, along with mashed potatoes and spinach, or some other green vegetable.

Chicken in Peanut Sauce

You have to be nuts to enjoy feeding a family. When you think of the hours spent in the kitchen cooking and washing-up, not to mention the time spent dragging the granny-cart around the market or manhandling rogue trolleys through the supermarket, joy and ecstasy are not words which spring to mind.

Yet, oddly enough, there is a profound maternal pleasure in that final ritual when they swarm to the table and enthusiastically wolf down the end product of those labours.

Not that it's a long-lasting sort of buzz. Food is eaten much faster than it's prepared. Where large lads are concerned, one has to cast a pretty swift verbal lariat to catch a dish-washing aid before they've all dashed off to some urgent diversion. That's the time when one is left thinking: 'Well, I'm glad they liked it and I know they're well nourished, but why am I still in the kitchen? I must be nuts!'

It was during one of these melancholy ponders that it occurred to me that it had been ages since this nut cook had cooked nuts in any shape or form. How silly of me. Nutty dishes are not only nice, but need not strain the budget. So I invested in a jumbo jar of crunchy peanut butter and went nuts in the kitchen – to the delight and appreciation of males large and small.

2 KG CHICKEN PIECES
2 TBSPN OIL
2 CLOVES GARLIC, CRUSHED
1 LARGE ONION, CHOPPED
3 TSPN MILD CURRY POWDER
1 TSPN TURMERIC
1/2 TSPN PAPRIKA
SALT TO TASTE
A TEASPOON OF CHILI (OPTIONAL)
3 CUPS CHICKEN STOCK
4 TBSPN CRUNCHY
   PEANUT BUTTER

Fry chicken pieces in the oil until golden and remove from the pan. Replace with the garlic and onion and fry until onion is translucent. Stir in the spices, then the stock and the peanut butter. Combine these ingredients well as they heat, then return the chicken to the pan, cover and simmer for 30–45 minutes until the chicken is thoroughly cooked. Serve with white rice and cucumber slices.

Occidental Soy Chicken

This dish is a boon to the cook on the run.

1 KG CHICKEN PIECES
2 CUPS CHICKEN OR
   VEGETABLE STOCK
¼ CUP MUSHROOM SOY SAUCE
¼ CUP CORNFLOUR
WATER AS REQUIRED

Trim chicken pieces and place in a saucepan with the stock and sauce. Simmer until chicken is cooked through. Remove chicken and bring the sauce to the boil. Boil for 10 minutes to reduce then turn down the heat. Mix the cornflour with water and stir into the sauce, stirring and cooking until it has thickened. Return the chicken to the sauce to coat well before serving on top of coconut rice.

Coconut Rice

3 CUPS COLD WATER
2 CUPS RICE
DASH OF SALT
¾ CUP SULTANAS
⅓ CUP TOASTED COCONUT

Place water, rice, salt and sultanas in a heavy-bottomed saucepan with a close-fitting lid. Bring to the boil, then turn off and allow to rest for at least 20 minutes so all the water can be absorbed. Do not remove the lid in that time. Thereafter, carefully stir up the rice with the side of a fork and blend in the coconut.

Rabbit

*C*hristmas traditionally is a time for catching up with rellies. The House of the Raising Sons, usually quite full enough without rellies, came upon some lost and other previously unencountered rellies this festive season. They were terrific – and blew away the cynical nuclear family thesis of 'you're born with relatives but you choose your friends'. Suddenly, we're all over the place, foraging for our roots. To that end, I hauled out the book of Schilling history – the only branch of our family that, to my knowledge, has done the complete genealogical thing from 1847 onwards. The boys were thrilled to discover that they're related to almost the entire wine-making Barossa Valley and much of the fruit-growing Riverland. But I quietly had the willies. The Schillings had a score of no less than 4712 living descendants within 140 years. Now that number of rellies represents one grandfather alone. We all had four grandparents. That's nearly 19,000 living rellies! Double it to include the in-law rellies and that's some big turkey one needs for an extended family Christmas dinner. Amazing how mankind breeds. That's the last time I ever say anything derogatory about the fecundity of rabbits. Unlike the rabbit on the Australian landscape, this is a very unusual dish. Do not be discouraged by the strange sound of it. It's very cheap, it goes far with rice or, better still, mashed potato and it's stunningly delicious.

For tender, tasty rabbit, it's a good idea to marinate the meat for a few hours, or even a few days, in vinegar and water.

In this case, the bunny needs only a few hours because the vinegar is neat.

Vinegar Rabbit

1 RABBIT, JOINTED
500 ML WINE VINEGAR
3 TBSPN BUTTER
500 ML THICK CREAM
2 BAY LEAVES
4 CLOVES
SALT AND PEPPER

Marinate the rabbit in the vinegar for a couple of hours, then, reserving the vinegar, dry the rabbit pieces and fry in the butter. When the rabbit is brown, add about two thirds of the vinegar, cover loosely and cook on a medium heat for about 45 minutes, or until the rabbit is becoming quite tender. Season well and add all the other ingredients. Simmer uncovered for 30 minutes and serve with rice or mashed potato, to soak up the delectably piquant cream sauce.

'Regular' Rabbit

3 TBSPN BUTTER
4 LARGE ONIONS, CHOPPED
2 CLOVES GARLIC, CRUSHED
6 BIG CARROTS, SLICED
1 RABBIT, CHOPPED INTO
    SERVING PORTIONS
2 TSPN GROUND BLACK PEPPER
1 1/2 TSPN SALT
1 STUBBY BEER
1 PKT PITTED PRUNES, SOAKED
    FOR AN HOUR IN 300 ML WARM
    WATER
3 OR 4 WHOLE CLOVES

In a large ovenproof casserole, melt the butter and gently fry the onions, garlic and carrot. Roll the rabbit in the salt and pepper, then ease in under the vegetables and cook lightly on all sides before turning up the heat and pouring in the beer a few moments later, then the prunes and water they were soaked in. As soon as it's beginning to bubble, cover with a fitted lid and bake in the middle of a 180° C oven for two to three hours. Serve with rice or mashed potatoes.

Irish Rabbit

When I was a child, rabbit meat was cooked for cats. 'Underground mutton' they called it and left it disdainfully in the frugal memories of the Depression years. Not so the Europeans. Living overseas I swiftly discovered scores of treatments for those huge, cultivated bunnies – and often wondered at the irony of my country leaving an excellent food source untapped in plague proportions.

While my boys have been reared on regular doses of rabbit, many of their friends, members of the perpetually hungry horde that miraculously materialises at mealtimes, have displayed, dare I say, almost rabbit-like timidity at the idea of eating this delicate game. It's never crossed their suburban path. Over the years, I've made a lot of converts. And I'm always finding new things to do with a meat that is as versatile as it is cheap. Introductory favourite, Irish roast rabbit, is a snuggle-up-to-the-fireside, easy and homely recipe. It's not a roast and it's absolutely not kosher. But it is delicious, served with a mound of creamy mashed potato.

1 RABBIT, CHOPPED INTO
   SERVING PORTIONS
2 LARGE ONIONS, CHOPPED
2 RASHERS OF BACON, TRIMMED
   AND CHOPPED (OR A SOUP
   SPOON OF SOYA BACON BITS,
   SOAKED)
300 ML SKIMMER MILK
3 TO 4 TBSPN CHOPPED PARSLEY
2 TBSPN BUTTER
FLOUR, SALT AND PEPPER

Drain and pat dry the soaked rabbit pieces and toss in seasoned flour before browning in the butter in a frypan. Place the browned rabbit pieces into a casserole, throw on the onion, bacon and parsley pour over the milk and bake at 190° C for a good hour.

Mustard Rabbit

This is the king of rabbit dishes.

10 OR SO PIECES OF RABBIT, SOAKED IN WATER AND VINEGAR
2 TBSPN PLAIN FLOUR, SEASONED WITH SALT AND PEPPER
2 TBSPN OLIVE OIL
2 TBSPN BUTTER
4 RASHERS OF BACON, DICED
5 SHALLOTS, FINELY CHOPPED
BOUQUET GARNI
3/4 CUP DRY WHITE WINE
3/4 CUP CHICKEN STOCK
1 TBSPN ENGLISH MUSTARD
1 TBSPN DIJON MUSTARD
1 CUP THICK CREAM

Having drained rabbit pieces from the water and vinegar soak, pat dry and then toss in the seasoned flour. Heat butter and oil in a large, heavy-based pot and then sauté the rabbit pieces along with the bacon. When lightly browned, add shallots, bouquet garni, wine and stock. Bring to boil. Reduce heat to a low simmer, cover and cook gently thus for 40 minutes or so. Lift out rabbit pieces with a slotted spoon and keep warm in a covered bowl. Skim the sauce and then whisk in the mustards and cream. Check seasoning. Return rabbit to the pot. Heat and serve with mashed potato.

Taking time for a leisurely stroll...

doesn't necessarily cost a cent...

but can leave one to feel...

like a million dollars.

Meat – With Renovations and Random Acts of Kindness

Meat had to endure a reputation as a decidedly subversive food for a long time in the House of the Raising Sons. All it takes is one vocal vego and meat's name is mud.

Meat does not have a good name at all. Think about it. Do we ever use the word 'meat' in a complimentary fashion? An idiot is a 'meathead', a fool is a 'silly sausage' or a 'pork chop', Rubanesque people are derided as 'meaty', pickup joints are 'meat racks', strip joints are 'flesh pots' . . . and so it goes on. Poor old meat! Oh well, you can't defame the dead.

However, there is a lot to be said for meat. I always worried that my vegos were not getting the essential elements they needed from meat, and so over-dosed them in compensatory mushrooms. There is something to be said for all that old 'feed the man meat' business. Meat should be a part of our regular diet. We are omniverous and, let's face it, there are some wonderful things you can do with meat!

Lamb

Lamb Pilaf

The old guilt trip. It works every time. Guilt is the best tool children have against their parents and they know exactly how to use it. They seem to wield that recriminatory weapon by instinct.

Who shows them how? Certainly, I was no role model for my pack. I am a failed guilt-wielder. The slightest suggestion that any one of them might not have borne the burden was always met with an indignant: 'Are you trying to give me a guilt trip?'

Children know even better than we that what they are supposed to have is love, support and endless endorsement. Guilt is bad for them. Making your kid feel bad is 'child abuse'. Any teenager will tell you that. But what about mums? There is no protective rule. Kids are within their rights to make us feel absolutely rotten. Which is how I felt on return from overseas – just as soon as the gifts had been dispersed.

So much for all the protective arrangements for my absence! The poor things. Even in their twenties they suffer without mum around. Do you know how difficult it is to remember which is rubbish night? How ghastly it is to live with a rampaging doberpuppy? And do you know how awful it is to have fried rice every night?

Oh, crushing shame! I was feeling desperately guilty. How did lads growing up amid all the varied food of the House of the Raising Sons end up being unable to think of more than one dish to cook every night?

They obviously needed to share in the cooking process. To that end, I summoned number one to the kitchen to help with a new and interesting way he could deal with rice. A delicious lamb pilaf! As I chopped the onions, I set him to browning the meat. At the first sizzle, the phone rang.

I took over with the meat. I finished the meat. I put on the onions. Took off the onions. Just as I was putting the dish in the oven, he came back – and announced he was going out. He really enjoyed the pilaf when he came home at 1 am. He said it was especially good reheated and that he hoped I would cook it again.

1 KG LAMB, BONED AND DICED
4 TBSPN MARGARINE
2 ONIONS, HALVED AND
　FINELY SLICED
1/4 TSPN GROUND CINNAMON
1/2 TSPN GROUND BLACK PEPPER
2 CUPS UNCOOKED RICE
1 CUP (OR MORE) SULTANAS
SALT TO TASTE
3 1/4 CUPS VEGETABLE OR
　BEEF STOCK
1/4 CUP LEMON JUICE
3 TBSPN SLICED, TOASTED
　ALMONDS
SPRINKLE OF CHOPPED PARSLEY

Saute the lamb in margarine until lightly browned and then remove. Place onions in the same pan, add cinnamon and pepper and fry until tender. Then butter a casserole dish and layer with meat, rice, sultanas and onions. Sprinkle salt on top and pour on the stock. Cover and bake for about an hour at 180°C. Remove the cover and sprinkle with lemon juice and almonds. Bake for another 15 minutes and serve, sprinkled with parsley.

Mutton Dressed as Lamb

A slow but tasty dish for a cheap cut.

1 1/2 KG CHOPS OR STEWING
　CUTS OF LAMB
4 TBSPN OLIVE OIL
JUICE OF 3 LEMONS
SALT AND PEPPER TO TASTE
1 GLASS WARM WATER
2 TSPN DRIED OREGANO
1 TSPN ROSEMARY

Place meat in a heavy casserole with a good lid and add oil, lemon, salt and pepper. Toss well, cover well and cook in the oven at about 170°C for half an hour. Thereafter open and add the water and herbs. Seal up again and cook for an hour – by which time the meat will be tender and juicy and surrounded by a nice lemon oil base. Serve with chips fried in olive oil, a green salad and crusty bread.

Sherried Lamb

An excellent recipe which virtually cooks itself while one frenzies away à la domestica.

1 KG DICED LAMB
ABOUT 1½ CUPS DRY SHERRY
WATER AS REQUIRED
SALT AND PEPPER TO TASTE
1 TSPN POWDERED CUMIN
OIL AS REQUIRED
2 CLOVES GARLIC, CRUSHED
2 LARGE ONIONS,
   FINELY CHOPPED
2 TBSPN PLAIN FLOUR

Marinate the lamb overnight in half a cup of sherry and enough water to cover. This tenderises the meat. Drain it well, pat dry and sprinkle with salt, pepper and cumin. Fry to brown and seal on all sides in the oil. Remove from the pan and fry the garlic and onions. When they are opaque, add the flour and fry some more until the mixture is browning. Return the meat to the pan and add the remaining sherry. Mix well, cover and simmer, stirring occasionally to prevent sticking, for a good two hours until the onion/flour/sherry mix is glutinous. Serve with sauteed potatoes and a salad.

Mince

All-in-one Dinner

Forget babies. Having a young doberman in the house is more work by far. And more expensive. I never knew a baby who could demolish an entire garden, for instance. And show me a baby who can gnaw a hole straight through a carpet to the back webbing, shred a plastic bucket and a dozen pine cones throughout the house and then scratch the paintwork clean off the doors.

To call this doberpup a handful is an understatement. He is a full-time job. He wants human attention. Nuzzle, nuzzle, prod, prod ... scratch, scratch, bark, bark, bang-a-bang-a-bang, howling ululation.

It is hard to get anything done for the noise and pestering. But it's harder by far when there is silence. Silence equates with stark fear. A quiet puppy is a looming disaster zone. Oh yes. Quiet puppy has been found in my bed, chomping on my best pillows. Quiet puppy has been found contentedly dismembering the couch upholstery. Quiet puppy has even been found neatly tearing the pages, one by one, from my current reading matter.

A lot of time has to be devoted to entertaining and tiring large doberpuppies – as a measure of urgent domestic economy.

Which is how the all-in-one meal came to pass. This is the ultimate time-saving domestic repast. It also is an excellent way to deal with the stray vegetables that didn't quite make it into other, more organised dishes.

1 KG LEAN MINCE
1 ONION, FINELY DICED
1 CLOVE GARLIC, CRUSHED
2 TSPN WORCESTERSHIRE SAUCE
1 TSPN CHILI POWDER (OR GOOD
   SAVOURY CHILI SAMBAL
   OR SAUCE)
SALT AND PEPPER TO TASTE
4 CUPS COOKED RICE
250 G MUSHROOMS, SLICED
ABOUT 3 CUPS ASSORTED
   LIGHTLY COOKED VEGETABLES –
   BROCCOLI IS GOOD,
   SO ARE DICED CARROTS,
   RED CAPSICUMS, BEANS,
   CABBAGE …
1 BOTTLE ITALIAN TOMATO
   COOKING SAUCE
GRATED CHEDDAR CHEESE
   AS REQUIRED
A SPRINKLE OF PARMESAN

Brown the mince with the onion and garlic and add the Worcestershire sauce, chili, salt and pepper. Place the rice in the bottom of a large pyrex or baking dish, cover with the mushrooms, then the vegetables, then the mince. Pour Italian sauce over the top, then cover with cheese and bake for about 30 minutes at 180°C.

Pea Kima

The old 'if you can't stand the heat, get out of the kitchen' bit might be an option for politicians – but not for parents. Not that you hear us complain, even in the inevitable Aussie heatwave.

In the cause of providing for our ever-hungry broods, we have to bite the proverbial bullet and keep on cooking, since even a humble potato salad begins with heat treatment on the spuds. Talk about full steam ahead in the kitchen.

There comes a point when things simply can't get any hotter, so who cares? I cope by swapping the pinnie for a simple sarong, which I regularly wring out with cold water and retie around myself.

Indeed, whenever cooking in sauna conditions, I'm reminded of the millions of fellow domestic cooks in India, Indonesia, Malaysia and Thailand – and am glad of my Western kitchen.

Just as Asian cooks have age-old skills in providing good food on minimal budgets, so have they accomplished the art of creating foods to counteract the effects of the tropical climate. Their spicy chili dishes heat up the body, make it sweat and thus make the air feel cooler – evaporative air-conditioning nature's way.

So it's curry I cook in the heat. And it's been doing the trick nicely.

I must admit I've not been indulging in any of those dishes that require complicated spice grinding. Quick and easy curry is the go at the height of summer. Keep it simple and liven things up with side dishes, I say.

This mince curry has been a lifelong favourite with the meateaters of my male mob. There are many delicious versions of this dish but this one, I believe, leans toward the Pakistani.

2 LARGE ONIONS, FINELY
    CHOPPED
4 TBSPN OIL OR BUTTER
1 KG LEAN MINCE
3 MEDIUM TOMATOES,
    ROUGHLY CHOPPED
1 HEAPED TBSPN MILD TO
    MEDIUM CURRY POWDER
1¹/₂ TSPN PAPRIKA
1 TSPN CHILI POWDER
    (MORE IF YOU LIKE IT HOT)
SALT AND BLACK PEPPER
    TO TASTE
1 TSPN GARLIC SALT
2 PINCHES OF CAYENNE
1 CAN OF PROCESSED PEAS

Saute the onions in oil until soft, then add mince and fry for a few minutes to break it up smoothly before adding tomatoes and stirring a few minutes longer. Toss in all the other ingredients, including the liquid from the can of peas. Amalgamate well and allow to simmer for an hour or so.

Red Lentil Dhal (recipe page 88) goes pleasantly with this dish, as does my favourite carrot curry – not that it's a curry. Exotic Carrots (recipe page 89) is really a fresh herb dish. The herbs I've used have varied greatly according to the time of year and what's flourishing in the garden. Mint, basil, tarragon, marjoram, parsley … they're all goers in almost any proportion. Don't be timid. Recipes don't have to taste the same every time they're cooked.

Red Lentil Dhal

1 CUP DRIED RED LENTILS
2 TBSPN VEGETABLE OIL
1 LARGE ONION, FINELY CHOPPED
4 CLOVES GARLIC, CRUSHED
2 CM FRESH GINGER, GRATED
1 TSPN TURMERIC
1 TOMATO, SKINNED AND
  FINELY CHOPPED
1 CARROT, SLICED THINLY
1/4 TSPN CHILI POWDER
BLACK PEPPER TO TASTE
1/2 TSPN GARAM MASALA

Wash lentils and drain. In a heavy-bottomed saucepan, heat the oil and fry the onions, garlic and ginger until the onion is light brown. Stir in the turmeric, tomato, carrot, chili and the lentils before adding the water. Boil for a few minutes and then turn the heat to medium and cook covered for half an hour before adding the remaining spices. Continue to stew until the carrots are soft and lentils are a nice, custardy mush. Serve with rice.

Exotic Carrots

1 BUNCH SPRING ONIONS,
   FINELY CHOPPED
1 TBSPN BUTTER
3 TBSPN FINELY CHOPPED
   FRESH MIXED HERBS
SALT TO TASTE
1 TSPN GARAM MASALA
1 1/2 TSPN TURMERIC
1 SCANT TSPN CHILI POWDER
CARROTS AS REQUIRED,
   PEELED AND FINELY SLICED
JUICE OF 1/2 LEMON

Fry spring onions in butter for a minute, add herbs and amalgamate well over the heat before stirring in all the dry spices. Reduce the heat to medium then add carrots. Toss them well in the mixture, then cover the saucepan and cook gently until they are tender. Stir in the lemon juice before serving.

Along with plain white rice, fresh-fried pappadums, chutneys and pickles, this meal is beautifully complemented with a little Indian salad. I make this one:

Indian Salad

1 LARGE CRISP ONION
1 LARGE FIRM TOMATO
2 TSPN DRY OR FRESH
   CHOPPED MINT
2 TBSPN WINE VINEGAR

Chop onion and tomato fairly finely, add mint and vinegar and allow to rest for about an hour before serving, stirring occasionally.

Meatballs

Spring should be beautiful and celebratory. We should be out sniffing the blossoms and rejoicing.

Instead, spring brings upon many of us the most awful involuntary reflex. We burst into a blooming frenzy of cleaning and purging. Instead of inhaling nature's sweet fragrances under the blue skies, we stay indoors sneezing in a cloud of dust and making an indescribable mess in the name of cleanliness.

It is very hard to explain. The best I can come up with is that I suddenly become possessed by masochistic spring madness. This does not altogether impress the House of the Raising Sons boys when I haul them out of the fresh air and into the cellar for a let's-throw-everything-out blitz.

They claim the madness is malevolently sadistic. I figure being considered insane is a small price to pay to get the job done. So I play out a demonic Linda Blair, revolving my head while grumbling boys lug a zillion pieces of domestic dross up the crumbling stairs and into the beautiful spring air.

But there's no such thing as a free lunch, let alone a free bunch of volunteers. Payback has to be a compulsory hearty dinner – heartier than usual. This homely peasant dish not only fills boy bellies but allows me to get on with assorted other chores while it's cooking. You know the syndrome. You just can't stop once you've started.

1 KG MINCE
2 EGGS
3 TBSPN FINELY CHOPPED
 PARSLEY
1 SMALL ONION, FINELY CHOPPED
SALT TO TASTE
1/4 TSPN CHILI POWDER
3 CANS TOMATOES, CHOPPED,
 WITH THEIR JUICE
1 TBSPN PLAIN FLOUR
1/2 CUP WATER

In a bowl, mix the mince with the eggs, parsley, onion and seasonings. Roll the meat into a dozen balls. Meanwhile, bring the tomato and juice to the boil. Pop the meatballs into the juices, cover and simmer for about 40 minutes. Remove the meatballs from the liquid and keep warm. Thicken the juice with the flour, mixed to pouring consistency with the water, and steadily stir in. Return the meatballs to the gravy and simmer for 10 or so minutes longer. Serve over white rice.

Beetburgers

I'm not big on canned foods, but the canning people were doing a promotion and this recipe included my favourite, beetroot. So I played around with it.

425 G CAN OF BEETROOT
 (SHREDDED IF YOU CAN
 FIND IT), DRAINED WITH
 THE LIQUID RESERVED
500 G LEAN MINCED BEEF
1/2 CUP BREADCRUMBS
1/2 TSPN CHILI POWDER
4 LARGE SPRING ONIONS,
 FINELY DICED TO THE TOP
1 LARGE EGG
SALT AND PEPPER TO TASTE
1/2 CUP WATER
3 TBSPN SAVOURY PLUM SAUCE

Combine the beetroot and the next six ingredients together in a bowl and shape into eight evenly sized meatball-shaped burgers. In a frying pan, bring the reserved beetroot liquid, water and plum sauce to the boil and then add the burgers. Simmer covered for about 15 minutes, turning the burgers half-way through. Serve with lashings of mashed potato along with shredded cabbage or green salad.

Trick-the-little-sods Burgers

Here is a recipe with which, for many years, I managed to trick pernickety youngsters into consuming lots of wholesome vegetable nutrition.

1 MEDIUM ONION
3 MEDIUM CARROTS
1 BUNCH PARSLEY
500 G TOPSIDE MINCE
1 CLOVE GARLIC, CRUSHED
1 CUP BREADCRUMBS
2 EGGS
1 TBSPN OLIVE OIL
SALT AND FRESHLY GROUND
    PEPPER TO TASTE
PLAIN FLOUR IF NECESSARY

Shred the onions in a food processor or grate them to a very fine dice (not mash). Also process the carrots to a fine mince-like consistency. Finely chop the parsley and mix all the other ingredients in a large bowl. Let the mixture stand for a few hours to absorb flavours and achieve a good consistency. If it seems at all sticky, some plain flour may be added. Flatten thin to patties and grill in the usual burger way, serving with fresh burger buns, melted cheese and salad or with mashed potatoes.

Caper-burgers

Mrs Worthington was well advised not to put her daughters on the stage. Had she also been told to keep herself well clear of the theatre, she'd have been even better advised. For mothers to spend their night backstage at a theatre after work is folly of the grandest order, or should I say disorder!

Never has the House of the Raising Sons been in greater chaos than when we all, bar one dog, became involved in a theatre production.

Instead of the acting members of the household coming home to late meals all laid out, hot and ready, we'd all burst into the kitchen together – and it was my challenge to devise 'instant' el cheapo meals for a ravenous pack of variable numbers.

The task was complicated by my having to duck through the huge and impatient males. Like the dogs, they can't help being underfoot when they're hungry and excited.

It was the merriest of hells. Loud voices, hilarious post mortems of the night's highs and hitches, snatches of song, argumentative exchanges about technicalities … all accompanied by the speed clatter of pots, pans and chopping board.

Remarkably enough, some rewarding new meals emerged from this pandemonium – proving that the tyranny of time is not all it's cracked up to be, and that fast food can be good food.

These American-inspired burgers were a major hit with the Raising Sons and rising stars, none of whom expected the fresh and interesting new flavours. They are a delicate and tasty meat patty, a bit like a cooked steak tartar, which I serve with steamed new potatoes, carrots, cabbage and a mustard and turmeric-seasoned white sauce.

You can either pre-make the meat mixture and let stand until ready, or do it all at once while the vegies are cooking. Either way, this is a brilliant new addition to the old mince repertoire.

1 KG MINCE
100 G JAR CAPERS, DRAINED
3 TBSPN CHOPPED PARSLEY
1 CLOVE GARLIC, CRUSHED
1 LARGE ONION, FINELY CHOPPED
2 EGGS
SALT AND BLACK PEPPER
   TO TASTE
1/2 CUP MILK
DRY BREADCRUMBS
   AS REQUIRED
BUTTER AS REQUIRED

Mix the mince, capers, parsley, garlic, onion, eggs, salt, pepper and milk thoroughly in a bowl. When ready to cook, shape quantities of the mixture into medium-sized balls, roll in breadcrumbs and fry in hot butter until lightly browned on both sides.

Cabbage Beef Casserole

Renovations – what a nightmare. The darling boys of the House of the Raising Sons took it upon themselves to upgrade the house's shabby old hall. They started with a vengeance, full of zeal and assumed expertise. Each had had a little association with some aspects of do-it-yourself, or so they claimed. I wondered what aspects.

The hall swiftly came to resemble a Village People gig. Bare-chested boys were up ladders with paintbrushes. Ponytails and head scarves were adopted. Chisels and spatulas, dustpans and buckets littered the floor amid the piles of decorator detritus.

The boys sizzled paintwork with heat guns. They ripped up carpets, hammering, sanding – and playing extremely strident 'work' music at full volume to be heard over the raging power tools.

Waging war on the pernicious clouds of dust, I sought places to hide. But there was nowhere. The kitchen was a disaster zone, deafeningly close to the action. Furthermore, its door chose this time to protest. Once shut, it would not open from within. And, what with the music and the hammering and the power tools, there was no hope of my bids to escape being heard by anyone.

So, marooned in a sea of raucous chaos and upheaval, I cooked to sustain the energies of these wondrous workers. The tricky thing was finding recipes for which all ingredients were already present – for there was no way out of the kitchen to renew supplies.

Thus was this American recipe a godsend. A very cheap, simple and wholesome mass-feeding dish which recharged the batteries in the diligent boys most effectively – once they heard my plaintive imprisoned cries that dinner was ready. It is a sort of lazy person's cabbage roll dish. But there's no rolling.

1 KG MINCE
VEGETABLE OIL AS REQUIRED
2 LARGE ONIONS, CHOPPED
2 CLOVES GARLIC, CRUSHED
SALT AND BLACK PEPPER
  TO TASTE
2 CARTONS TOMATO PASTE
1 CUP WATER
1 CUP UNCOOKED
  LONG-GRAIN RICE
6 CUPS SHREDDED CABBAGE
SOUR CREAM AS REQUIRED

Brown the beef thoroughly in the oil, draining off any fat. Add the onion, garlic, pepper, salt, tomato paste and water and bring to the boil. Then add the rice, cover and simmer for about 20 minutes. Place half the cabbage in a broad-based casserole. Pour in the meat mixture. Top with the rest of the cabbage, cover and cook at 180°C for about an hour. Serve with dollops of sour cream on top. Mashed potato is a nice accompaniment.

Cheat's Stroganoff

This is ridiculously easy.

600 G SKIRT STEAK
3 TBSPN BUTTER
1 LARGE ONION, FINELY CHOPPED
SALT AND FRESHLY GROUND
  BLACK PEPPER
2 TBSPN TOMATO PUREE
1 SMALL TIN (1 CUP) EVAPORATED
  MILK
2 TBSPN DRY SHERRY

Cut the meat into fine slivers about 3 cm (1 inch) long. Melt butter in a non-stick frypan and fry the onion until it is soft and translucent. Remove onion from the pan and pop in the meat, stirring to brown on all sides. Season liberally with salt and pepper and return onion to the pan along with the tomato puree and evaporated milk. Reduce the heat, stir well, cover and allow to simmer for about 40 minutes before adding the sherry and continuing to simmer for another 15 minutes. Serve with ribbon egg noodles and a light and leafy side salad.

Shepherd's Pie

A hush fell upon the House of the Raising Sons. Bombastic boys softened their ways. The thumping techno music pulsed comfortingly rather than stridently. Kindly gestures emerged from the preoccupations of youth – a certain welcoming tidiness, flowers, offered coffees and innumerable awkwardly angular hugs.

One lad even created a lovely art work and hung it in the hall to touch the spirit with love and trust. Such was the boys' reaction to bereavement.

No one could ever dare to tell me that these lads are not cherubs, albeit with a hormone problem. They may be chaos to live with but, when the chips are down, they come up trumps.

And thus, so do I, for there is nothing more soul-restoring in times of sorrow than homely, old-fashioned comfort food. The very normality of the process of cooking is therapeutic. Food is that life force – the business of continuity which blends pleasure and comfort with the necessity of sustenance.

Preoccupied as I had been, though, there had been little mental space for culinary inspiration. So it is not surprising that when I saw a tasty-looking shepherd's pie arrive on the Daw House Hospice meal tray, I promptly stole the idea for one of our domestic repasts.

Shepherd's pie is perfect invalid food as well as hearty working-body fare, one of the few traditional Anglo-Saxon dishes that serves well on all fronts. It is soft in texture and strong in energy provision.

There are many variations on the theme of a shepherd's pie. One can improvise all over the place. Technically, it should be lamb mince, leaving cottage pie to be the ground beef variation. But such subtleties are long since lost in Australia and I don't think it really matters. That it is filling and delicious is all. This is my variation on the theme – made to economy and flavour rather than to the specifics of tradition. For invalid fare, it should perhaps be a little more bland.

2 ONIONS, FINELY DICED
1 CLOVE GARLIC, CRUSHED
BUTTER AS REQUIRED
1 KG MINCE
1 SMALL CAN CONDENSED
   TOMATO SOUP
1 TBSPN WORCESTERSHIRE
   SAUCE
1 TBSPN DRY SHERRY
2–3 TSPN POWDERED MUSTARD
2 TBSPN FINELY CHOPPED
   PARSLEY
1 BEEF STOCK CUBE IN
   1/2 CUP WATER
CORNFLOUR IF NECESSARY

TOPPING:

4–5 LARGE POTATOES, PEELED
OPTIONAL (BUT DELICIOUS)
   350 G PUMPKIN, PEELED
BUTTER AS REQUIRED
SALT AND PEPPER TO TASTE
1 EGG, BEATEN

Fry the onions and garlic in the butter until translucent, then add the mince and brown thoroughly, stirring frequently to ensure it has no lumps and the moisture evaporates. Add the tomato soup, Worcestershire sauce, sherry, mustard, parsley and stock. Simmer this mixture steadily until it seems thick. If you are rushed, mix cornflour with a little water, stir in and cook as a thickening agent. Preferably, let the meat reduce naturally, then season to taste and place in the bottom of a goodly sized casserole dish. While this is cooking, boil the potatoes (and pumpkin) and mash with butter, salt and pepper. Mix in the egg and spread over the meat mixture. Bake for about 45 minutes in a 180–200°C oven until the top is browning.

Mince Crust Pie

A funny old recipe. I can't recall how or when it came into my hands, but it goes down a treat with boys of all ages.

CRUST:
500 G GOOD MINCE
1½ CUPS BREADCRUMBS
1 GLASS DRY WHITE WINE
2 TBSPN CHOPPED PARSLEY
2 TSPN DRIED MUSTARD POWDER
1 TSPN CELERY SALT
SALT AND BLACK PEPPER
   TO TASTE
1–2 EGGS

Mix all ingredients and allow to stand so that flavours absorb. Then press the mixture into a well-greased medium pie dish, rounding up the mince sides.

FILLING:
5–6 MEDIUM POTATOES, GRATED
1 SMALL TO MEDIUM ONION,
   GRATED
1 GREEN CAPSICUM,
   DICED FINELY

Blend ingredients together, pouring off potato juices, and pack into the centre of the mince pie lining.

TOPPING:
25 G MELTED BUTTER
1–2 TSPN WORCESTERSHIRE
   SAUCE
SALT AND PEPPER TO TASTE
50 G GRATED CHEDDAR CHEESE

Drizzle butter all over the top and add a few drops of Worcestershire sauce here and there, salt and pepper, and then cook in a 190°C oven for 40 minutes. Remove and add the covering of grated cheese. Cook for another 10 minutes until the cheese is just brown. Remove and allow to cool slightly.

Mince Casserole

This is really a variation on meatloaf.

MEAT MIX:
1 KG LEAN MINCE
1 MEDIUM ONION, FINELY
   CHOPPED
2 CLOVES GARLIC, CRUSHED
2 CARROTS, GRATED
1 CAPSICUM, GRATED
DASH WORCESTERSHIRE SAUCE
1 TSPN MUSTARD POWDER
SALT AND BLACK PEPPER
   TO TASTE
3 TBSPN CHOPPED PARSLEY

REST:
4–5 MEDIUM POTATOES, PEELED
   AND SLICED
1 HALF-SIZED TIN TOMATO SOUP
WATER AS REQUIRED
1 CUP DRY BREADCRUMBS
1 CUP GRATED CHEDDAR CHEESE

Thoroughly combine all the meat mix ingredients, and allow to rest for a while to absorb flavours while you prepare the spuds. Choose a deep casserole dish and, greasing the base and sides, place a layer of potato on the bottom and then a layer of the meat mix. Repeat until the ingredients are used up. Mix the tomato soup with the same quantity of water and pour over. Then sprinkle with the breadcrumbs and cheese, cover and bake for two hours in a slightly slow oven, about 160°C.

Ground Beef Noodle Bake

The big secret to this dish is the use of Philadelphia cream cheese – a very
American ingredient.

2 PACKETS EGG THIN NOODLES,
   COOKED
100 G SOFT CREAM CHEESE
1/2 CUP EVAPORATED MILK
3 TSPN LEMON JUICE
1/2 TSPN GARLIC SALT
2 TSPN WORCESTERSHIRE SAUCE
1 MEDIUM ONION,
   FINELY CHOPPED
1 GREEN CAPSICUM,
   FINELY CHOPPED
1 TBSPN BUTTER
1 KG MINCE
1 CARTON TOMATO PASTE
2/3 CUP ITALIAN TOMATO SAUCE

Into the still-warm cooked noodles, mix the cream cheese, evaporated milk, lemon juice, garlic salt and Worcestershire sauce. Place in the base of a large, greased baking dish and firm down. Soften the onion and capsicum in butter in a frying pan and add the mince, cooking until well browned. Then stir in the two tomato sauces and stir until reduced. Spread over the top of the noodles and bake in a 180°C oven for 15–20 minutes.

Soaking in a hot tub is great for

ironing out one's tensions...

but take care not to wrinkle ...

the birthday suit...

Oxtail

Alan's Oxtail

You either love or hate oxtail. My family has always loved it and always presented it in the traditional British Mrs Beeton way. We gnaw on the gelatinous bone tips religiously in the belief that it strengthens nail and hair – not that science has ever really confirmed this. But no winter is complete without at least one oxtail stew.

I was uttering such sentiments to the butcher when he asserted that he cooked the best oxtail in the business. And it wasn't à la Beeton.

With that he scribbled this recipe down on butcher's paper and wrapped the oxtail in it. That night as the oxtail was bubbling contentedly away in the oven, I heard the fire engines wailing in the distance. Little did I suspect that the fire they were attending was that very butcher's shop. It never re-opened. And I have never seen Alan again to tell him what a triumph his dish is.

2 OXTAILS, JOINTED
CORNFLOUR AS REQUIRED
SALT AND FRESHLY GROUND
BLACK PEPPER TO TASTE
SWEET SHERRY AS REQUIRED
ONIONS, SLICED
CARROTS, SLICED
ANY OTHER VEGETABLES
YOU CHOOSE

Trim the oxtails thoroughly, roll them in seasoned cornflour and place side by side in one layer in a shallow casserole dish. Pour over sherry to almost but not quite cover the oxtail. Cover with foil or a lid and place in the centre of a slow-to-medium oven (120–150°C) for at least two hours. Then open the top and add your chosen vegetables. Sliced onions and carrots are my choice, but Alan says he adds everything from peas to cauliflower as well. Re-cover and replace in the oven for another two hours – or more if it's convenient. Serve in bowls with crusty bread or, if you prefer, on a bed of rice.

Sausages

Smyrna Sausages

With enough flair, a novel mince meal is good enough to put in front of dinner guests. Here's an adaptation of a ripper recipe, gleaned almost a lifetime ago from a Greek friend.

SAUSAGES:
QUANTITY OF TRICK-THE-LITTLE-
SODS BURGER MIXTURE
(PAGE 92) MINUS THE CARROTS
1 TBSPN FRESHLY GROUND
CUMIN SEEDS
1 TSPN VINEGAR
OLIVE OIL AND BUTTER
AS REQUIRED

SAUCE:
2 MEDIUM ONIONS,
CHOPPED FINELY
MARGARINE AS REQUIRED
6–8 MEDIUM TOMATOES,
SKINNED AND CHOPPED
(A LARGE TIN OF TOMATOES
CAN BE SUBSTITUTED)
1 SMALL TUB OR CAN OF
TOMATO PASTE
1 BAY LEAF
SALT AND FRESHLY GROUND
BLACK PEPPER TO TASTE
A LITTLE WATER TO DILUTE

Add the cumin and vinegar to the burger mixture. Mix it thoroughly and let stand overnight if possible. Roll out palmfuls of the mince mixture into small sausage-like shapes and fry in a half-and-half mixture of hot olive oil and butter until the sausages are well browned. Place them in an oven-proof casserole to keep warm.

Glaze onions in margarine. Add tomatoes and other ingredients, except the water. Simmer slowly over low heat until it has achieved a thick sauce-like consistency – about half an hour should do. Add water if it looks too thick. Pour the sauce over the sausages in the casserole and keep warm in the oven. Serve with flat egg noodles and grated cheese.

Baked Spicy Snags

No parent should ever stay away from home on New Year's Eve. In my case, it was unavoidable one year. So I crossed my fingers and toes and put all the boys on trust. Well, there wasn't a boy in sight when I returned home on New Year's Day. Just the odd sonorous snore from behind closed doors.

But boy, oh post-pubescent boy! Was the house radiant in its cleanliness and neatness. Sparkling. Pristine. I knew immediately. It must have been some party!

There is no more tell-tale sign of rampant, absentee-parent partying than a truly scrubbed house. The cleaner the house, the wilder the party. Of course, the parent is not supposed to notice. You are assumed to have astonishing levels of stupidity – and complete amnesia about your own diabolical youth.

But there are signs. For instance, the dawn hour munchies had depleted the fridge of almost everything except a few tired salad vegetables. Replenishing the fridge would never have occurred to hungover boys on a desperate cleaning frenzy. Indeed, the first they noticed was about 4 pm on New Year's Day when they were groping some coffee together to go with the morning-after panadol and discovered we were milkless. By which time mum was watching their discomfort with some high degree of amusement.

Poor dears had no memory of where the milk had gone – let alone the food supplies. Clearly, the dog had done it, whatever it was. No recriminations. I was not angry. Just a bit compromised since New Year's Day is not the best day for shopping.

Thus it was that we ended up with humble old snags for dinner that night. Boring old BBQ snags don't have to be plain fare. They are extremely receptive to some improvisational jazzing up. I have been surprised to find how many people never think of embellishing sausages. Nifty variations on standard themes are invaluable in a busy household.

Sausages may be baked in the oven with almost any sauce addition – from diluted plum sauce to jars of Mexican salsa. Each variation delivers a new lease of life to a snag.

For cheap emergency tucker, baked sausages are hard to beat.

1¹/₂ KG PLAIN SAUSAGES

SAUCE:
1 JAR ITALIAN TOMATO
   COOKING SAUCE
1 CAN SWEETCORN NIBLETS
2 TSPN CHILI PASTE
   (OR CHILI POWDER)
1 TSPN GROUND CUMIN
¹/₂ CUP WATER

Mix sauce ingredients well and pour into a baking dish. Prick and lay the sausages in the sauce, cover the dish with foil and bake in a 180°C oven for 90 minutes. They're nice served with sauteed potatoes, or even rice works well as an accompaniment.

Baked Mushy Snags

A Saturday bargain buyer's special, this one. Cheap end-of-the-week mushrooms and very ordinary snags.

2 CLOVES GARLIC, CRUSHED
500 G OR MORE MUSHROOMS,
   SLICED
BUTTER AS REQUIRED
2 TSPN MIXED HERBS
¹/₂ CUP CREAM
SALT AND PEPPER TO TASTE
¹/₂ CUP WATER
1¹/₂ KG PLAIN SAUSAGES

Saute the garlic and then mushrooms in the butter with the herbs until the mushrooms are softened. Mix in the cream and seasonings and puree. Dilute with water and place in a baking tray. Add the sausages and cook in a 180°C oven for 90 minutes.

Schnitzels

Serving Up Schnitzels

It strikes me that schnitzels are like the McDonald's of Germany – the commonplace, cheap dish with the universal appeal. Of course, they're different in Europe where officially they're made from delicate young veal – the most cruelly reared of all meats.

But in Australia butchers slap 'em out with a bit of beef and the kids love them. I can never go wrong cooking schnitzels. They're a popular request dish at the House of the Raising Sons and, because of the beating and flattening of the meat, they make little meat go a long way. They're classic economy food. However, between you and me, they're a bit on the dull side. No wonder the Italians jazzed them up with cheeses and sauces.

I like to vary the theme with internal coatings – and I prefer using chicken fillets to meat.

I can't get a consensus from the ever-ravenous boys on one favourite. The younger ones seem to like the peanut best. The older ones like mustard. I like the basil and parmesan. These are nifty variations because they turn dreary schnitzels into interesting food, and they are the happiest made hours in advance and kept in the fridge until cooking time – after which they seem to disappear from the boys' plates with greedy intensity.

One kilogram of chicken cooked this way and served with vegies will feed a tribe, or, in more civilised households, a table of eight to ten quite generously. Chicken breasts should be sliced through the centre, and then halved and each piece delicately pounded just a bit, though it's not essential since chicken is already delicate.

Apart from the flavour dips, the technique is the same for all three variations. After covering with flavouring, the chicken pieces must be rolled thoroughly in breadcrumbs and, after resting to absorb the flavours, pan-fried in hot pure vegetable oil until they're golden and crispy on the outside.

(These quantities are enough for four schnitzels.)

BASIL AND PARMESAN SCHNITZEL:

3 TSPN CHOPPED BASIL
2 TBSPN GRATED PARMESAN
1 EGG YOLK
1 TBSPN CREAM

MUSTARD SCHNITZEL:

2 TBSPN MILD MUSTARD (I LIKE
    TO MIX GRAIN AND SMOOTH
    MUSTARDS)
2 EGG YOLKS
2 TBSPN CREAM

PEANUT SCHNITZEL:

2 TBSPN SMOOTH PEANUT PASTE
2 TBSPN SOY SAUCE
1/2 TSPN CHILI POWDER
1 EGG YOLK

In all cases, mix the ingredients to a smooth consistency and then dip the chicken pieces, ensuring that they're well coated all over before dipping in dried breadcrumbs and patting firm. Fry in oil until golden brown and the chicken is cooked through. Serve with french fries or creamed potatoes and vegetables of choice.

There are certain battles ...

to be fought over ownership...

if one is to eat ...

the fruit of one's own labour...

Veg Out

Suddenly I had a full-on vegetarian in the house. There was no warning. No 'I am planning to stop eating meat' or 'I don't believe in eating animals'. There was just an abrupt announcement at dinner one night: 'No meat for me. I'm a vegetarian!'

Not wishing to scathe my hard-earned reputation as a 'cool dude' mum, I uttered an all-knowing 'as you wish darling', and re-jigged the dinner portions, thinking sullenly that this was the price I paid for sending him to an alternative free-thinking school.

It doesn't take long for the family cook to realise that the introduction of a vegetarian to the house is going to complicate meals. One can't make a vego feel like a second-class citizen by giving them only a proportion of the varied evening's repast. And, since I like both vegetables and challenges, the culinary game became finding vego meals so interesting and satisfying that the carnivores did not know that they were being deprived of meat.

Erika's Vegie-burgers

This is the ultimate poverty tucker dish. Just a few carrots and onions and parsley, really. Sometimes I add odd variations, if there is one zucchini or one capsicum hanging around looking lonely in the crisper. Never be afraid to improvise.

4 MEDIUM CARROTS
2 LARGE ONIONS
1 BUNCH PARSLEY
2 EGGS
4 CLOVES GARLIC, CRUSHED INTO
  A PASTE WITH A LITTLE SALT
  AND NUTMEG
OATMEAL AS REQUIRED
SALT AND FRESHLY GROUND
  BLACK PEPPER TO TASTE
FLOUR AS REQUIRED
BUTTER AND OIL AS REQUIRED

In a food processor or using a hand-grater, grate the carrots and onions. Finely chop the parsley. Mix in a bowl with eggs and garlic then add enough oatmeal to gain a sticky mince consistency, seasoning with salt and pepper according to taste or dietary requirements. Add flour to make the mixture smoother and easier to handle before moulding into flat hamburger patties no more than $1^1/_2$ cm thick. Sizzle in hot butter and/or oil. Serve with a side salad and creamy mashed potatoes flavoured with chopped chives. The burgers are also nice cold.

Winter Chili Beans

Another bottom-of-the-fridge special. Go for it with whatever you find.

700 ML BOTTLE ITALIAN
  TOMATO SAUCE
1 LARGE ONION
ASSORTED VEGETABLES TO
  HAND SUCH AS:
  2 CARROTS, DICED
  2 CELERY STALKS, SLICED
  1 CUP CAULIFLOWER FLORETS
  1 CUP CHOPPED MUSHROOMS
4 CLOVES GARLIC, CRUSHED
1 TSPN CHILI POWDER
1 TSPN GRATED NUTMEG
DASH OF SOY SAUCE
1 TSPN PAPRIKA
1 TSPN DRY BASIL
500 G RED KIDNEY BEANS
  (SOAKED FOR 24 HOURS AND
  THEN BOILED IN SALTY WATER
  UNTIL TENDER AND STRAINED;
  OR TWO LARGE CANS OF
  PREPARED BEANS)
SALT AND BLACK PEPPER
  TO TASTE
GRATED CHEDDAR CHEESE
  AS REQUIRED

Warm the tomato sauce in a heavy-based saucepan and add the vegetables and spices. Stew until vegetables are almost tender, then add the strained, cooked beans and stew a while longer. Season with salt and pepper to taste. Add more chili if you like and sprinkle with grated cheddar cheese. Serve with a share bowl of cornchips.

Cheese Lentil Casserole

A warm, wintry dish which doesn't mind turning up on a spring or autumn menu. It can be served alone, but it's nice as a dish in a larger meal.

250 G BROWN LENTILS
WATER AS REQUIRED
1 LARGE ONION, FINELY CHOPPED
2 CLOVES GARLIC, CRUSHED
2 TBSPN BUTTER
1 BIG CARROT, FINELY CHOPPED
1 STICK CELERY, CHOPPED
1 CUP STOCK OR WATER
130 G SMALL MUSHROOMS,
    SLICED
1 CUP BREADCRUMBS
    (PREFERABLY BROWN)
2 TBSPN CHOPPED PARSLEY
2 EGGS
1 SMALL CARTON COTTAGE
    CHEESE
PINCH OF CHILI
SALT AND PEPPER TO TASTE
2 CUPS GRATED CHEDDAR
    CHEESE
HANDFUL OF SESAME SEEDS

Boil lentils in very salty water until cooked, then drain. Meanwhile, fry onions and garlic in butter. Add carrot, celery and stock. Cover and simmer until almost cooked. Add mushrooms for a couple of minutes, then drain the mixture. Thoroughly mix all ingredients except for one cup of the cheddar cheese and the sesame seeds. Pack into a shallow greased casserole dish, coat with the rest of the cheese and sprinkle with sesame seeds. Bake for about 45 minutes at 180°C until cheese is golden.

Real Bubble and Squeak

Every family has its own version of this old English classic. But since I bore two boys in England, I reasoned that I owed them the truth of their geographic heritage – or something like that. Perhaps I just like it because it's still the best of all Sunday breakfasts. The quantities are really up to you. Fifty–fifty spud and cabbage is the idea.

2 TBSPN BUTTER
1 MEDIUM ONION, CHOPPED
2 CUPS COOKED POTATO
2 CUPS FINELY DICED, LIGHTLY
  COOKED CABBAGE
SALT AND PEPPER TO TASTE

Melt the butter in a frying pan, then fry the onion until it begins to caramelise (turn brown). Meanwhile, mash the potato and mix in the chopped cabbage. When the onion is ready, press the potato mixture on top of it in the pan and firm down with a spatula. Let it sizzle on between moderate and high until a golden brown crust forms underneath, then carefully cut into sections, ease up and turn over to cook a crust on the reverse side. It should then have a cake-like appearance and be ready for a liberal seasoning and to be served with eggs, sausages or whatever takes your fancy.

Brussel sprouts can be substituted for the cabbage and any other cooked vegetable leftovers added.

Pastryless Pies

Since pastry-making is laborious and pastry-buying is extravagant, I've been on a bender making pastryless pies. It's hard to know what odd urge brings on these bouts of compulsive kitchen experimentation. I've always believed that motherhood brings with it an internal nutritional mechanism which steers me, via mysterious personal cravings, to buy and prepare what turns out week by week to be a pretty well copybook balanced diet. I never go shopping with a list of required vitamins, minerals and fibres – but somehow it always works out. If it's not some sort of primary instinct, then I'm darned if I know how I do it.

Suddenly we don't need pastry, however wholesome, in our diets. My body clock has ordained that it's time for alternative pies.

Ever tolerant of the unexpected, the male mob masticated merrily through these variations of pastryless pie. I serve them with a side salad, lightly perked up with a lemony vinaigrette. For the record, that's been the source of our living C and A vitamins.

Potato Crust Pie

CRUST:
4–5 BIG POTATOES
SALT, PEPPER AND NUTMEG
    TO TASTE
1 TBSPN BUTTER

Cook and mash potato, incorporating seasonings to taste. Generously butter the inside of a 25 cm pyrex or baking dish and then line it with the potato, pressing it down and around the sides firmly. Allow this to cool and dry slightly while preparing the filling for which you can use any vegetables of your choice.

FILLING:
3 TBSPN OLIVE OIL
2 ONIONS, CHOPPED
1 EGGPLANT (CHOPPED, SALTED,
   DRAINED, WASHED AND
   SQUEEZED OUT)
2 RED CAPSICUMS, CHOPPED
4 SMALL ZUCCHINIS, SLICED
2 TOMATOES, CHOPPED
1 FRESH CHILI, SLICED
200 G MUSHROOMS, SLICED
SALT, PEPPER AND PAPRIKA
   TO TASTE

TOPPING:
2 EGGS
$2/3$ CUP YOGHURT
$1/3$ CUP MILK
4 TBSPN GRATED PARMESAN

Heat oil in a heavy-based frying pan, add onions and fry until translucent. Add eggplant, followed by the capsicums. Lower the heat, cover and cook for 15 minutes. Then add chopped zucchinis, tomatoes and chili. Cover and stew together for 30 minutes. Then add mushrooms and cook, uncovered, for another 10 minutes. Season generously and then, using a slotted spoon to drain excess fluid as you go, transfer the cooked vegetables to the potato crust.

Beat eggs into yoghurt and milk and pour over the vegetables. Sprinkle the parmesan on top and bake in a 180°C oven for about an hour – until the top is golden. Allow to cool slightly before serving. A little chili sambal served on the side adds excitement for those who seek it.

Cauliflower Potato Crust Pie

CRUST:
2 CUPS GRATED RAW POTATO
1/2 CUP GRATED ONION
SALT TO TASTE
1 TBSPN PLAIN FLOUR
1 EGG WHITE, LIGHTLY BEATEN

FILLING:
1 TBSPN BUTTER
1 LARGE ONION, CHOPPED
2 CLOVES GARLIC, CRUSHED
1 TSPN CHOPPED BASIL
1/2 TSPN DRIED THYME
1/2 TSPN CHILI POWDER
SALT AND PEPPER TO TASTE
1 MEDIUM CAULIFLOWER,
   CHOPPED SMALL
1 CUP (OR MORE) GRATED
   CHEDDAR CHEESE
2 EGGS
1/4 CUP MILK
SPRINKLE OF PAPRIKA

Combine crust ingredients and pack firmly around the edges of a well-greased 20–23 cm pie dish or shallow casserole. Bake in a 190°C oven for about half an hour. Brush the crust with a little oil, bake for another 10 minutes and remove. Meanwhile, heat the butter and fry the onion and garlic for a few minutes. Add the herbs and seasonings (except paprika) and mix well, then toss in the cauliflower, stir thoroughly and cover. Cook on medium heat for 15 minutes until the cauliflower is tender. Then spread half the cheese on the pie base, pour on the cauliflower mix and then the rest of the cheese. Beat the eggs into the milk and pour over the cauliflower. Sprinkle with paprika and bake for about 40 minutes – until the eggs are well set.

Asparagus and Broccoli Delight

The first days of spring are like turning the lights on in a teenager's room. The place looks a shocking mess in the bright glow. One new spring morning I came home lugging ten tonnes of weekend shopping, and was appalled at the sight of our back garden in the cheerful illumination of the sun.

Everything seemed ragged and overgrown. Leaves and cedar berries littered the corner sitting sanctuary. Spiders' webs lattice-worked the garden chair bases. Weeds had sprouted in the stonework and the herb pots. Nothing less than fence-to-fence shambles.

The garden looked desperate, its disarray so indecently exposed in the serene sunshine. But I had indoors to do. The shopping to unpack, beds to strip, washing to put on, cooking to get under way . . .

Then I remembered the boys. They used the garden much more than I. They sat for whole summer nights under insect lamps playing cards in the sitting sanctuary.

I followed a susurrus of voices and found several lads gathered around coffee mugs enjoying the weather on the front verandah. One was strumming languidly on a guitar. Not a worry in the world. They had been there since they got up, they said. Midday? I didn't dare to ask. Such a beautiful afternoon, they enthused. So nice to sit outside at last. Who could disagree? But why weren't they sitting under the trees out the back where they usually sat? Oh, no, they had thought of that, one volunteered stupidly. But this was much cleaner. Hadn't I noticed that there was a mess out the back? Nobody would want to sit out there.

Well, you have never seen happy, relaxed faces drop so quickly. Dark looks were glanced at the outspoken fool who had walked them straight into the work trap. The astonishing thing was how quickly the boys had the job done. Many hands make light work. I'd barely finished organising in the kitchen when they had downed tools with a sense of achievement.

Thus it came to pass that on that night I cooked the boys of the House of the Raising Sons a summery outdoor dinner, which they took to consume in their favourite warm-weather haunt in the sheltered corner of the garden.

The meal was a radiant success and rightly so. This vegetable dish was a celebration in itself – a celebration of asparagus which was in season and even quite cheap.

2 BUNCHES OF ASPARAGUS, CUT INTO 4 CM LENGTHS
1 LARGE HEAD OF BROCCOLI, CUT INTO SMALL FLORETS
2 TBSPN VEGETABLE OIL
2 TBSPN LIGHT SOY SAUCE
1 CHICKEN OR VEGETABLE STOCK CUBE
5 TBSPN WATER
1 TBSPN DRY SHERRY
1 TBSPN CORNFLOUR
PINCH OF GROUND GINGER
PINCH OF CHILI POWDER

Steam the vegetables until they are cooked, but still firm. Warm the oil in a pan. Mix all the other ingredients together and add to the oil, stirring until the sauce has thickened properly – and then cook a little longer. Add the vegetables to the sauce, heat thoroughly so the vegetables are fully coated, and serve with rice.

a pair of concealed hands…

Broadie Loaf

Broad beans, known in some places as fava beans, have been my lifelong favourite vegie. The fact that the Raising Sons also adore broadies means that I have to shell and peel the most massive quantities to mask my own greed for them.

I suspect broad-bean passion is a genetic phenomenon. My grandfather grew, he bragged, the best broadies in suburbia. He liked to eat them big and floury. He liked to suck out the inner flesh and discard the skins. My father rather preferred them young and tender – in large quantities. He was happy with just a plate piled with broadies as a meal. I carry on the tradition. I love cooking the tops of the plants, nipped out mid-growth to bring on the bulk of the beans. It is like a delicate, broad-bean flavoured spinach. I also like the baby beans cooked whole, as well as the beans themselves. So, after a lifetime of seasonal broadie-gorging, it was a delight to encounter a new recipe.

400 G SHELLED AND COOKED
  BROAD BEANS
225 G SAUSAGE MEAT (OPTIONAL)
1 EGG
3 TBSPN DRY BREADCRUMBS
1 MEDIUM ONION, FINELY
  CHOPPED
2 TSPN BUTTER
1 TBSPN CHOPPED SAGE AND
  SAVORY OR 1 TSPN DILL,
  1 TBSPN PARSLEY AND
  ½ TSPN PAPRIKA
SALT AND PEPPER TO TASTE
3–4 HARD-BOILED EGGS

Puree the beans, and mix in the sausage meat, raw egg and breadcrumbs. Fry the onions in butter until they're translucent and add to the mixture along with the herbs, salt and pepper. Grease a loaf tin and line the base with about 1 cm of the mixture. Place the shelled boiled eggs in a line down the middle and then pack the rest of the mixture in tightly around them, smoothing and rounding the top. Cook this upright in a baking tin of water in the centre of a 180°C oven for an hour. Let it cool before attacking it.

Chinese-style Broad Beans

A fresh approach to an old vegie. This one's a consistent winner.

2 TBSPN OIL
1 TSPN SALT
500 G SHELLED YOUNG
   BROAD BEANS
WATER AS REQUIRED
4 SPRING ONIONS, FINELY
   CHOPPED

Heat oil in a frying pan, add the salt and then sizzle the broad beans for about two minutes before adding enough water to cover. Cook until broadies are tender. Drain. Toss thoroughly with the finely chopped spring onions and serve.

Green Beans

I'm always mad for fresh green salad. But beans are reasonably priced and I've found several ways to vary the flavour. One nifty shortcut, if one saves the basil crop and makes pesto before the cold weather comes, is to toss cooked green beans in a tablespoon of pesto sauce. Yummy.

Another pleasant variation to give beans a whole new zing, especially if they're being served in a bland meal context, is this mixture, enough for 500 g of chopped, hot, cooked beans:

2 TSPN READY-MADE MUSTARD
1 TSPN WORCESTERSHIRE SAUCE
SALT AND BLACK PEPPER
   TO TASTE
1/4 TSPN CHILI POWDER

Mix the lot together and toss it through the beans.

Sauerkraut Barossa Valley Style

For a celebrational German-style meal, serve this with frankfurters, mashed potatoes and German mustard. These ingredients should be judged according to your own numbers and taste. For one whole cabbage, use about five bacon rashers or, for a vegetarian dish, a handful of soya bacon chips soaked in warm water.

1 CABBAGE
WATER AS REQUIRED
1 LARGE ONION, FINELY CHOPPED
1 TBSPN BUTTER
5 BACON RASHERS, CHOPPED
JUICE OF 2–3 LEMONS
1 TBSPN RAW SUGAR
SALT AND PEPPER TO TASTE
CARAWAY SEEDS TO TASTE

Finely slice the cabbage and cut into lengths of about 2 cm. Wash and then blanch it well in boiling water. Meanwhile, fry onion in butter, add bacon and cook gently until the bacon is well cooked and the onion tender and transparent. Add the well-blanched cabbage, stir, and then pour in the lemon juice and sugar. Incorporate thoroughly and allow to stew gently for 30 minutes. Stir occasionally. The cabbage should be tender but not soggy. Add salt, caraway seeds and lots of freshly ground black pepper and adjust the lemon–sugar balance according to taste.

Chinese Cabbage

The Chinese have a cabbage alternative which is ridiculously easy, quick to prepare and tasty as a side dish.

1 CABBAGE
2 TBSPN VEGETABLE OIL
SALT TO TASTE
1 TSPN SUGAR
2 TSPN SOY SAUCE
5 TBSPN WATER

Slice cabbage into strips of about 1 x 3 cm. Heat oil and stir-fry the cabbage with the salt for a minute or so. Add the other ingredients and cook for five minutes. That's it.

Cheesy Spinach

I was in love with this dish the first time I tried it at my friend Brenda's place. It is a regular House of the Raising Sons special served with almost any meal. Silverbeet, or chard, can also be used.

1 BUNCH SPINACH
BUTTER AS REQUIRED
3 FAT CLOVES GARLIC, CRUSHED
5–6 EGGS, BEATEN
1 CUP GRATED CHEDDAR CHEESE
1 CUP DRY BREADCRUMBS
SPRINKLE OF PAPRIKA

Wash, de-vein and lightly cook the spinach. Butter a shallow casserole dish, spread the spinach in it and incorporate the garlic as evenly as possible. Pour on and integrate the eggs, then spread the cheese, then the breadcrumbs on top of that. Sprinkle with paprika and bake in a 180°C oven for 30–40 minutes until the egg has set and the top is golden.

Stewed Leeks

There is absolutely no better way to cook leeks. This slow-cook method in a heavy pot veritably 'melts' them and even those who purport not to like leeks come back for seconds.

BUNCH OF LEEKS
1 TBSPN BUTTER OR MARGARINE

Slice meticulously washed leeks crosswise in 1 cm lengths. Melt butter or margarine in the bottom of a heavy-based saucepan. Place the sliced leeks on top. Put a well-fitting lid on the saucepan. Cook on low heat so the leeks can slowly stew and soften, which will take about an hour. Half-way through, lift the lid and give the leeks a stir to ensure even cooking. They should emerge much reduced in volume but delicate and tender. Cooked this simple but slow way, they're perfect with roasts, or almost anything.

Glazed Beetroot

Beetroot is a much unappreciated, old-fashioned vegetable. But it's very wholesome and given this alternative treatment, it acquires a whole new zing.

1 TBSPN GOOD MARMALADE
1 TBSPN GRATED ORANGE OR
    LEMON PEEL
1 TBSPN ORANGE OR
    LEMON JUICE
BUNCH OF BABY BEET, COOKED
    AND PEELED

Warm the marmalade with the peel and juice in a pan and then add the beetroot, rolling and sizzling them until they are well coated and the mixture is glazing on them. Good with turkey or ham.

Capsicum Crop Glut

Here are some secrets from my Mediterranean friends.

Italian Pure Capsicum Stash

ANY AMOUNT OF RED
   CAPSICUMS, DE-SEEDED
SALT AND PEPPER TO TASTE
OLIVE OIL AS REQUIRED

Slice the ends of the capsicums so they can stand up. Stand in a roasting tray and cook in a 200°C oven until the tops are blackening. Move them around, testing the bases for softness. Cook until well done. Before cold, strip the skins from the outside, slice and either: season, oil and eat; season and store in the fridge in olive oil; or package up and freeze for later use.

Greek Capsicum Preserve

1 KG RED AND GREEN
   CAPSICUMS
SALT TO TASTE
WINE VINEGAR AS REQUIRED
1–2 LARGE CARROTS,
   VERY FINELY SLICED
6–10 CLOVES GARLIC,
   FINELY SLICED
4 TBSPN PARSLEY,
   FINELY CHOPPED
PURE VEGETABLE OIL

De-seed and finely slice the capsicums and place in a bowl. Sprinkle liberally with salt, cover with vinegar and leave for twenty-four hours. Drain. Take several small jars or one large jar, wash and sterilise. Place a layer of capsicums, then a layer of carrots, then garlic, then parsley, then another layer of capsicums and so on until the jar is layered to the top. Pour on oil to cover, seal and store for up to a month.

Zucchini Tomatoes

People either love or loathe zucchini, aka courgette. The cook's challenge is to give the zucchini lovers the pleasure of the veggie while not having to cook something alternative for the zucchini haters. This dish turned out to be it. Everyone loves it.

ABOUT 400 G FRESH, FIRM
ZUCCHINI, CUT IN 1 CM SLICES
1 PUNNET CHERRY OR GRAPE
TOMATOES
1 SMALL CLOVE OF GARLIC,
CRUSHED
2 TBSPN BEST OLIVE OIL
SALT AND FRESHLY GROUND
BLACK PEPPER
SPRINKLE OF CHOPPED BASIL

Heat oil in large frying pan, quickly sizzle garlic and then pour in the sliced zucchini and sauté them enthusiastically until most pieces are golden on both sides. At this point, throw in the whole carton of little tomatoes and stir around well. Leave them there until they are starting to pop. Then add a sprinkle of chopped basil, plenty of salt and pepper and serve.

Short-cut Black Beans and Rice

It was really more about music than food. The boys were in something of a Cuban music reverie and I, foolishly, mentioned that Cubans ate black beans and rice. Suddenly, there was no dish the boys had ever wanted more. Cuban food with Cuban music, the complete immersion. Well, don't tell them, but I did not go the whole hog. Instead, I did a short-cut impression – which turned out to be so moreish that I have done it again and again.

1 ½ CUPS JASMINE RICE
2 TBSPN OLIVE OIL
1 MEDIUM RED ONION, FINELY CHOPPED
2 STALKS CELERY, VERY FINELY DICED
1 SMALL GREEN PEPPER, VERY FINELY SLICED
1 MEDIUM RED PEPPER, VERY FINELY DICED
3 FAT CLOVES GARLIC, MINCED
2 (OR EVEN 3) 400 G CANS BLACK BEANS, DRAINED
2 TBSPN WHITE WINE VINEGAR
½ TSPN CHILI POWDER
1 TBSPN CHOPPED FRESH OREGANO (OR 1 TSPN DRIED)
PLENTY OF SALT AND PEPPER

Cook the rice and let it rest while preparing the vegetables. In a frying pan, heat the oil and sauté the onion, celery and peppers until the pepper skins are starting to soften. Toss in the garlic and stir well before adding the beans and vinegar. Bring to the boil, cover and turn to low for about 10 minutes. Then add the rice, chili and herbs, blending thoroughly. Season before serving either as a side dish with dinner meats or as a lunch with crispy salads and lots of Mexican-style chili sauce.

Spicy Sambal Mushrooms

Mushrooms can be a bit bland and predictable. Here's a way to pep them up.

3 TBSPN VEGETABLE OIL
3 CLOVES GARLIC, CRUSHED
1 TSPN CHILI POWDER (OR MORE DEPENDING UPON TASTE)
CHILI SAMBAL (AS MUCH AS YOU DARE)
500 G BUTTON MUSHROOMS
SALT AND PEPPER TO TASTE
2 TBSPN LIGHT SOY SAUCE

Heat the oil, sizzle the garlic very briefly and then add the chili powder and sambal. Stir these well into the oil and lower the heat. After two minutes, add the mushrooms and toss well in the oil mixture. Add salt and pepper to bring out the juices, stir, and cover to cook on a medium heat for about five minutes. Add the soy sauce and serve with rice.

Maple Yam

This recipe comes from the wilds of cyberspace, provided by Louve, an American Indian Shaman. The American Indians introduced the sweet potato to the Pilgrims. Yams were essential to the Pilgrims' survival, and the vegetables are an important part of the American celebration of Thanksgiving.

1 KG SWEET POTATOES
WATER AS REQUIRED
250 G MELTED BUTTER
1 CUP MAPLE SYRUP
1 TBSPN BRANDY
A FEW WALNUTS AND RAISINS, CHOPPED

Boil sweet potatoes, plunge into cold water and peel. Place in a lightly greased baking dish and toss with butter, maple syrup and brandy. Top with raisins and walnuts and bake at 180°C for 45 minutes until golden and caramelised. Serve with turkey or ham.

Fried Green Tomatoes

Another recipe given over the Internet when I expressed curiosity after seeing the movie of the same name.

6 GREEN TOMATOES
SALT AND PEPPER TO TASTE
1 LARGE EGG, BEATEN WITH
    2 TBSPN MILK
1 CUP SELF-RAISING FLOUR
1 CUP FINE POLENTA OR PLAIN
    FLOUR
1 CUP VEGETABLE OIL

Wash and slice tomatoes to a thickness of about 1 cm. Salt and pepper them, then dip into the beaten egg and milk before rolling in the mixed flour. Place the tomatoes in the hot oil and sizzle until golden brown on both sides. In the American tradition, green fried tomatoes are served with Southern Fried Chicken (see recipe page 57).

Cheezee Pumpkin

My cheeseaholic tribe cope enthusiastically with cheezee pumpkin as a main course, although in less punishing times it is better as a rich side dish with meat.

BUTTER AS REQUIRED
1½ KG PUMPKIN, PEELED
1 CUP CREAM
SALT AND PEPPER TO TASTE
2½ CUPS CHEESE – HALF CHEAP
    CHEDDAR, HALF PARMESAN
    OR PECORINO

Butter a casserole dish. Slice pumpkin to 1 cm thickness and place in layers. Drizzle well with cream, generously salt and pepper and then thickly cover with the grated cheeses. Bake for an hour at 180°C. Serve with green salad and crusty bread.

Granny's Tatty Salad

An earthy Irish summer recipe.

4 HUGE SPUDS, BOILED IN
   THEIR SKINS
1 BIG GRANNY SMITH APPLE,
   PEELED AND FINELY DICED
1 MEDIUM ONION,
   VERY FINELY DICED
2 BOILED EGGS, FINELY CHOPPED
1 TBSPN CHOPPED PARSLEY
A FEW HEFTY DOLLOPS OF MAYO
SALT AND PEPPER TO TASTE

Peel and chop the boiled spuds. Place the potatoes, apple, onion, eggs and parsley in a salad bowl, mix in the mayo, season and refrigerate.

Carrot and Quark Salad

There's nothing as celebratory and aesthetic as a fresh carrot dish amid the salad choices of a summer spread.

2 HEAPED TBSPN QUARK
   (OR RICOTTA)
2 TBSPN LEMON JUICE
1 FAT CLOVE GARLIC, CRUSHED
HANDFUL OF CURRANTS
SALT AND FRESHLY GROUND
   BLACK PEPPER TO TASTE
250 G CARROTS, GRATED

Combine the quark, lemon juice, garlic, currants, salt and pepper and mix to a smooth paste. Mix in the carrots and chill.

Tasty Onion Salad

I can't stand people who make a fuss about eating onions. Onions are superbly nutritious and utterly delicious. Not only that, they are cheap. This dish is one of the reasons why there is no lad in the House of the Raising Sons who has any sort of challenged attitude towards onion-eating.

4 MEDIUM-SIZED ONIONS
  (BROWN OR WHITE)
2 TBSPN SALT
2 TBSPN LEMON JUICE
1 TSPN WINE VINEGAR
3 TBSPN OLIVE OIL
DASH OF COLD WATER
SALT AND PEPPER TO TASTE
HANDFUL OF CHOPPED PARSLEY

Peel onions, halve them and slice finely. Put them in a colander, pour the salt over them and work it in with your hands until the onions are smooth and briny. Rinse well under running water and put aside to drain. Mix the lemon juice, vinegar, olive oil, water and seasonings and then combine together with the onions and parsley in a bowl.

Maxwell.

a regular job guaranteed to have not a single volunteer...

No-frills Gado Gado

I've long been an avid aficionado of Indonesian cuisine which, because of its use of pungent ingredients, is not every Australian's idea of everyday tucker. Conditioned as they have been to exotic aromas from the kitchen, my mob grizzle if I dare to fry trasi, that particularly whiffy shrimp block so popular in Asia.

So here is an adaptation of Indonesia's wonderful cooked salad. This version omits the weird and wonderful bits and is easy and wholesome. It's delicious warm and fresh, but just as nice cold the next day. I make it in platter proportions and use whatever vegetables I have to hand.

3 POTATOES, DICED
4 CARROTS, SLICED
1/2 CABBAGE, SHREDDED
1/2 CAULIFLOWER IN FLORETS
200 G BEAN SPROUTS
4 HARD-BOILED EGGS, SLICED
3 LEBANESE CUCUMBERS, SLICED

Cook the potatoes and carrots, blanch the cabbage and cauliflower and immerse the bean sprouts in boiling water for one minute. Drain and cool and arrange all the ingredients on a platter.

SAUCE:
1 ONION, FINELY CHOPPED
3 CLOVES GARLIC, CRUSHED
1 TBSPN GRATED FRESH GINGER
1 TBSPN OIL
1/2–1 TSPN CHILI POWDER
1 TSPN BROWN SUGAR
JUICE OF 1/2 LEMON
6 TBSPN CRUNCHY
   PEANUT BUTTER
1/2 CUP COCONUT MILK
1 CUP HOT WATER
SALT TO TASTE

Fry the onion, garlic and ginger in the oil until the onion is translucent, then add chili and cook a little longer. Reduce the heat before adding the remaining ingredients, stirring constantly to blend well. The peanut butter will thicken and might need extra water to give it a creamy consistency. Do not let this sauce boil. Pour the sauce over the arranged vegetables and garnish with boiled egg and cucumber. Serve as a side vegetable dish or alone with white rice. If you want to add a touch of Indonesian authenticity, serve with fried prawn crisps or kroepek, a classic Indonesian accompaniment that can be found at Asian supermarkets.

Tabouli

This tabouli recipe came from my Palestinian friend, Emira. It's the real thing and I have never met its match. Tabouli will store for many days if kept well-sealed in the refrigerator.

1/2 CUP BURGHUL WHEAT,
    SOAKED OVERNIGHT
1 MEDIUM ONION,
    FINELY CHOPPED
2 BUNCHES OF CRISP PARSLEY
5 GOOD SPRIGS OF MINT
SPRIGS OF FRESH DILL
    (OPTIONAL)
2 FIRM TOMATOES
SALT TO TASTE
JUICE OF 3–4 LEMONS
2 TSPN OLIVE OIL

Drain the wheat then turn it into a tea-towel and squeeze thoroughly to remove all excess water. Mix the onion in with the wheat. Wash and finely chop the parsley, mint and dill. Cut the tomatoes into very small dice and add to the mixture. Then add salt, and pour on the lemon juice and olive oil. Mix thoroughly and check for taste.

Hoummus

Why pay a fortune for little tubs of hoummus when it is so easy and cheap to make at home. The only investment is the tahini, which keeps in the fridge for ages.

1 CUP OF CHICK PEAS, SOAKED
OVERNIGHT
WATER AS REQUIRED
2 TBSPN TAHINI
2 FAT CLOVES GARLIC, CRUSHED
JUICE OF 3–4 LEMONS
SALT TO TASTE
2 TSPN GROUND CUMIN
SPRINKLE OF PAPRIKA
OLIVE OIL AS REQUIRED

Drain the chick peas, which will have doubled in size. Place in a saucepan and cover with cold water. Boil for about an hour until chick peas are plump and soft. It is not possible to overcook chick peas but they can be undercooked. Drain chick peas, reserving a little of the water. Puree the peas in a blender, adding tahini, garlic and lemon juice. If still too thick, dribble in some of the reserved cooking water. Sprinkle generously with salt and add cumin. Check for taste before spooning into a deep bowl, garnishing with paprika, then sealing by pouring a layer of olive oil over the top. This will keep in the fridge for a week.

For a complete meal, buy a dry or wet felafel mixture from supermarkets and fry in oil. Serve with tabouli, tzadziki and hoummus.

Tzadziki

The big trick of a good tzadziki is to keep it from being sloshy. This is achieved by careful preparation of the cucumber.

1 CONTINENTAL CUCUMBER OR
  2 LEBANESE CUCUMBERS
SALT TO TASTE
2 LARGE CLOVES GARLIC,
  CRUSHED
1 CUP OF EUROPEAN-STYLE
  YOGHURT
SPRINKLE OF PAPRIKA

Wash and grate the cucumber with the skin on. Place in a sieve and sprinkle with a little salt. Drain for a few hours so the juices run out. Then, with very clean hands, squeeze the hell out of the cucumber so most of the high water content is gone. Place what remains in a bowl, then add garlic and yoghurt. Mix well, tasting for salt, and sprinkle paprika on top.

Guacamole

I have a passion for anything containing chili – and guacamole has always been one of my concepts of pure health food. Here's my version.

2 RIPE AVOCADOS
1 TBSPN GRATED ONION
1 CLOVE GARLIC, CRUSHED
2 FIRM TOMATOES, PEELED,
  SEEDED AND FINELY CHOPPED
JUICE OF 1 LEMON
SALT AND FRESHLY GROUND
  BLACK PEPPER TO TASTE
1/2 TSPN CHILI POWDER (OR MORE
  IF DESIRED)

Mash avocado flesh with a fork and then add all the other ingredients, mixing well. Cover and chill. An avocado stone in the mixture will prevent discolouration.

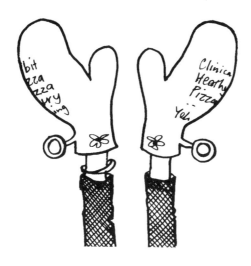

Marvellous Miscellanea

Ît's all very well to go out and buy fast foodie things, but when the household is large, takeaway or ready-made luxuries are beyond the budget. This does not mean, however, that such goodies are off the menu. They're all easy to make at home and, if one can rope in a few chatty helpers, they're fun to do. They are also significantly better than the bought counterpart!

Rarebit

For all the rough and tumble of their toddlerhood, at no stage did my sons wreak havoc upon my body in the way my huge baby doberman has done. For one thing, they never head-butted while hurtling at a million over-excited miles an hour.

The dark purple bruise on my left foot is there to stay, I think. That is the foot on which the dog likes to stand while I am cooking. The bruise is freshened up at regular intervals.

Dobermans love proximity. They like to feel their loved ones against their fur. They like leaning on people. And standing on tender bits of them.

The arrival of this dog in the House of the Raising Sons heralded a whole new cooking technique. There is the pinioned-to-the-corner-of-the-work-bench chopping pose, the one-legged-pivot-to-the-sink manoeuvre, the lateral-stretch-to-the-stove action, the dog-aerobic-extraction exercise to get to the cupboard . . .

This has given those heavy-stirring and standing-on-the-spot recipes a whole new appeal. Hence this absolute yummy from America, which also has the advantage of being one of those very simple, old-fashioned, everyone-loves-it goodies with a new-wave elegance of flavour. It is a form of rarebit – a cheese sauce which goes extremely well not only as a toast topping, with or without a poached egg on top, but over broccoli or cauliflower or, indeed, potatoes. It is guaranteed to send vegetarians into a delirium of delight.

If you don't have as good a reason as I do to stand still stirring in the kitchen, you can always make rarebit the lazy way. Rarebit is simply rather fancy cheese on toast. The better the cheese, the better the rarebit. The way to add zest is to butter toast and spread it with a little mustard (or horseradish) before covering it with cheese and melting under the griller. A poached egg on top makes the cheat's version of the famous buck rarebit.

2 TBSPN BUTTER OR MARGARINE
2 TBSPN PLAIN FLOUR
2 TSPN DRY MUSTARD
1 STUBBY OF BEER
250 G GRATED CHEDDAR CHEESE
1 TSPN HORSERADISH OR
    CHILI SAMBAL
1 CLOVE GARLIC, CRUSHED
SALT AND PEPPER TO TASTE

Melt the butter, sprinkle on the flour and mustard and stir quickly to a roux. Using a whisk, add in the beer, whisking briskly, and bring the mixture to the boil. Lower the temperature and simmer for a few minutes, stirring regularly. Add the remaining ingredients and stir some more until they are all amalgamated smoothly.

Fasta Pizza

There are no rules for the way in which you take this yummy shortcut to total household happiness. It's all an artistic smothering and covering game. Tinned or fresh pineapple may be added. Lots of meat, or none. Just play pizza bars at home.

TOMATO PASTE, THINNED WITH
TOMATO SAUCE
PITTA OR LEBANESE BREAD
(PREFERABLY POCKETLESS)
FRESH TOMATO
HAM/CHICKEN/SAUSAGE OR ANY
LEFTOVER MEAT
ONION
VEGETABLES OF CHOICE
(CAPSICUM, MUSHROOM, ETC.)
CHEESE – EITHER MOZZARELLA
OR A GOOD CHEDDAR CHEESE
OLIVES (OPTIONAL)
PEPPER (OPTIONAL)
CHILI (OPTIONAL)
HERBS (OPTIONAL)
PAPRIKA (OPTIONAL)

Spread the tomato paste mixture to the edges of the bread, but not too thickly or it will ooze. Then chop and add tomato, meat, vegies and anything else you fancy. If using mozzarella, it can be placed lower in the scheme of things, with sliced goodies decorating the top. If using good old cheddar, which is just as nice and some-what cheaper, it's best spread on the top, covered only with a sprinkling of olives, pepper, chili, herbs or paprika. Cook these pitta pizzas in a 180°C oven for 15 minutes.

Mayer's Clinically Healthy Pizza

These pizzas are limited only by your imagination and what is in the fridge. Children notoriously like ham and pineapple, men love lots of salami or wursts.

DOUGH:
2 CUPS WHITE FLOUR
1 CUP OATS
1 TBSPN DRIED YEAST
1 TBSPN VEGETABLE OIL
1 CUP OF WARM WATER

Mix the lot thoroughly and knead furiously (a dough hook on the Kenwood helps) then rest the dough for about an hour to rise. Roll out to 1 cm thickness and place on a flat, lightly greased baking tray. To give a crispy base, bake this for about five minutes before applying the goodies. If you like it a bit squelchy, don't. While the dough is rising, prepare the topping.

TOPPING:
1 CARTON TOMATO PASTE,
  THINNED WITH TOMATO SAUCE
3 BIG TOMATOES, CUT IN
  SMALL CUBES
1 LARGE ONION, FINELY SLICED
2 x 125 G TINS SARDINES OR
  1 x 250 G TIN SALMON
1 LEMON
200 G FINELY SLICED
  MUSHROOMS
DRIED BASIL AND OREGANO
  TO TASTE
FRESHLY GROUND BLACK PEPPER
  TO TASTE
500 G GRATED CHEAP CHEDDAR
  CHEESE

Spread sauce thinly on base and then load with tomatoes. Spread the onions around, drain the sardines and shred them about, squeeze the lemon over, layer with mushrooms, sprinkle with herbs and pepper and then coat the lot generously with the cheese. Cook in preheated 200°C oven for half an hour.

Pasties

Living overseas for years, one of the things I missed most about Australia was a really-truly pasty. Even the Cornish don't make them as well as we do. So there was nothing for it but learn to make them myself. They were a big hit. I ended up even serving them at dinner parties.

PASTY PASTRY:

This delicious pastry is a sort of shortcrust.

1½ CUPS SELF-RAISING FLOUR
PINCH OF SALT
75 G LARD
75 G MARGARINE
½ TSPN LEMON JUICE
½ CUP WATER

Mix flour and salt in a bowl and add the lard and marg in small pieces. Give these fats a gentle but rudimentary rub into the flour with the fingers – just a quickie – before adding the lemon juice and water and mixing it all thoroughly into a dough. If the dough gets sticky, add more flour. Let this dough rest in the fridge for 10 minutes before placing it on a floured surface and rolling it out long and thin. Fold it over end to end, then return it, wrapped in grease-proof paper, to the fridge for another 10–15 minutes. Do this a couple more times and then roll and cut it to the sizes required.

Circles cut with saucers make round-sided pasties and oblongs make square pasties and less wastage. Use some egg beaten with a little milk to moisten the edges of the pastry to help seal in the goodies. Pierce the tops with a fork and use it to seal down and decorate the edges. Brush the tops with the egg and milk mixture before placing the finished creations on greased and floured or grease-proof paper-lined baking trays and into a 180–200°C oven for about 30 minutes or until they are golden brown.

PASTY FILLING:
4 MEDIUM-SIZED POTATOES
3 CARROTS
1 SMALL TURNIP OR SWEDE
SLICE OF PUMPKIN
1 CUP PEAS
SALT AND PEPPER

Steam the vegetables, then dice them to 1 cm pieces. Mix everything together. Pack quantities of this liberally onto pieces of pastry and seal down.

CAULIFLOWER CHEESE PASTY FILLING:
1/2 CAULIFLOWER
2 MEDIUM ONIONS, CHOPPED
1 TBSPN BUTTER
SALT, BLACK PEPPER AND
   PAPRIKA TO TASTE
250 G CHEDDAR CHEESE

Slice finely down the florets and stems on the cauliflower and steam for a few moments until cooked but not mushy. Fry the onions in butter until browning. Mix with cauliflower, adding salt, black pepper and paprika. Pack this on to the pastry shape and then cover liberally with grated cheddar cheese before sealing down.

Cheang's Cheaty Sweet and Sour Sauce

This 'cheat' sweet and sour recipe can turn just about any bland food, from assorted steamed vegetables to pork, chicken and even cheap frozen fish fillets, into a smart repast.

2 CLOVES GARLIC, CRUSHED

1 THUMB-SIZED KNOB OF
  GINGER, GRATED

1 SCANT TBSPN VEGETABLE OIL

1 MEDIUM ONION, CHOPPED

3/4 CUP TOMATO SAUCE/KETCHUP
  (I PREFER HEINZ)

1 MEDIUM TIN CHOPPED
  PINEAPPLE (WITH JUICE)

WATER AS REQUIRED

2–3 TSPN SUGAR

HANDFUL OF FROZEN PEAS FOR
  COLOUR (OPTIONAL)

SALT TO TASTE

Briefly sizzle the garlic and ginger in the oil, add the onion and fry to translucent before pouring in the tomato sauce and pineapple pieces. Stir together, diluting with water to get the desired consistency. Sugar according to taste, starting with two teaspoons. Like salt, sugar is easier to add than to remove. Caution is the key word. Add peas and salt for piquance and simmer gently until ready to pour over stir-fried or steamed vegetables, chopped chicken meat or pork (dipped in salted cornflour and fried), diced cooked chicken, all served with steamed or even fried rice.

Honest Sweet and Sour Sauce

For purists who baulk at using bottled tomato sauce, here's another straight-forward sweet and sour recipe which requires a bit more effort in the stirring department. In this recipe all main ingredients are in equal quantities, so it's very easy to adapt proportions for large or small mealtime gatherings.

2 TBSPN SOY SAUCE
2 TBSPN ORANGE JUICE
2 TBSPN DRY SHERRY
2 TBSPN VINEGAR
2 TBSPN SUGAR
2 TBSPN TOMATO PASTE
1 TBSPN CORNFLOUR MIXED IN
   4 TBSPN WATER

Place all ingredients in a saucepan and bring to a medium-high heat, stirring constantly. You can tell when it's cooked because it will have thickened to a classic sauce consistency and the flour will have turned a rich clear colour. For variation you can add chopped spring onion, pineapple pieces, frozen peas, longitudinally diced cucumber, chopped tomatoes or shredded capsicums.

brush twice a day ... first the front

and then the back ... be careful and don't bite the dust!

Just Desserts

'Macaroon me on a dessert island!' sighed the lad, as he tucked into seconds of dessert. And, of course, that's why we push ourselves just that bit further and turn on the ever-popular 'afters' course. Appreciation! Everyone loves sweets. Well, almost everyone. Those who love them, love them enough to make up for the few salty-tooths who eschew them. In the House of the Raising Sons, desserts are a symbol of domestic contentment. All is right with the world when there is dessert on the table.

Apple Betty

This dish is traditionally cooked with white bread – but if you have any raisin loaf, it enhances the dish a treat.

BUTTER AS REQUIRED
12 SLICES WHITE BREAD
1 KG GRANNY SMITH APPLES,
    PEELED, CORED AND
    FINELY SLICED
1/2 CUP BROWN SUGAR
HANDFUL OF SULTANAS

Butter a medium-sized baking dish. Remove crusts, cut bread into quarters and butter generously. Line the dish with pieces, butter-side down. Then place a layer of apples on top, sprinkle with sugar and sultanas, and cover with another layer of bread. Do a last layer of apples with sugar and finish off with a layer of bread, butter-side up. Cover and bake in a 180°C oven for about an hour. Remove the cover for the last few minutes to ensure a lovely brown top. Serve with cream or custard.

Avocado Ice Cream

When avocados are bargain buys, this is a very alternative option. The lads thought they would hate it. They didn't. Surprise, surprise.

2 MEDIUM AVOCADOS
1/4 CUP SUGAR
1/3 CUP LEMON JUICE
PINCH OF SALT

Put the avocado flesh into the blender with the other ingredients and puree smooth. Pour into freezer trays and freeze for four hours. After the first two hours, take the mixture out and rewhiz it to ensure smoothness. Refreeze.

Baked Bananas

So often, the simplest things are the best. My mother, a lifelong banana-lover, used to make this dish whenever there was a surplus of bananas or, I suppose, whenever she was in the mood, since it was quite often. I love it now as I loved it then.

2 TBSPN BUTTER
2 TBSPN SOFT BROWN SUGAR
2 TBSPN LEMON JUICE
2 TBSPN BRANDY
4–5 RIPE BANANAS,
   CHOPPED IN HALF

Melt the butter with the sugar in a casserole dish. Add the lemon juice and brandy, then roll the bananas in the sauce and put the lot into a 200°C oven for about half an hour. Serve in the syrup with a dollop of whipped cream.

Quince Compote

Quinces are members of the rose family. There is no flavour quite like a quince; sweet and tart with a slightly grainy texture. When cooked they turn a lovely pink. A lot of people put quinces in the too-hard basket, but they really are worth the effort. This is the absolute all-original quince recipe.

1 KG QUINCES
1 CUP WATER
6 TBSPN WHITE SUGAR

Cut the quinces into eights, then peel and core them. Put the peel and core in water with the sugar and boil for half an hour to make sweet syrup. Remove the peel and core from the syrup, replace with the fruit pieces and simmer until they are soft. Then serve hot or cold with cream, ice cream, yoghurt or cereal.

Peach and Blueberry Cobbler

Nature has a criminal streak. It makes crops ripen all at once in a massive glut. Why can't it spin things out and allow us a chance to get through the crop?

The House of the Raising Sons is not equipped with much of a garden, but two elderly trees have loyally over-provided us with white-fleshed peaches year after year.

The boys go to exaggerated lengths to avoid doing the picking. So they were delighted when stormy weather had peaches thumping on the ground by the bucketload. Of course, windfall peaches last all of five minutes. The bruises set in and they are compost.

Wonderful as it is, eating peaches and cream for nightly dessert has its limits. So I thanked MIT, IBM, the US defence, Bill Gates, Telstra and the world of computer geeks as I headed into the Internet in search of peach options. The best solution came from the aptly named Peachtree City in Georgia. Nectarines are a good substitute for the peaches.

a sonny day in the garden...

3 CUPS PEELED AND SLICED
  RIPE PEACHES
2 CUPS BLUEBERRIES,
  FRESH OR FROZEN
1/4 CUP CORNFLOUR
2/3 CUP SUGAR
1 CUP FLOUR
2 HEAPED TSPN BAKING POWDER
1/4 CUP SUGAR
PINCH OF SALT
1/4 CUP QUICK OATS, UNCOOKED
1 TSPN GRATED LEMON RIND
1/4 TSPN CINNAMON
4 TBSPN BUTTER OR MARGARINE,
  THINLY SLICED
1/2 CUP MILK

Preheat oven to 200°C. Place fruit in a greased two-liter casserole. Combine the cornflour with the sugar and stir thoroughly through the fruit. In a separate bowl, combine the flour, baking powder, sugar and salt. Stir in the oats, lemon and cinnamon and distribute the slices of butter throughout the mixture. Add milk and stir until a stiff dough forms. Drop the dough in teaspoon sizes around the edges of the casserole and over the fruit. Bake for 30 minutes. Serve warm.

Blueberry Flummery

Why did flummery ever go out of fashion? Foolish food fads. This is a wonderful summer treat.

2 TSPN GELATINE
1/4 CUP COLD WATER
2 CUPS FRESH BLUEBERRIES
1/4 CUP SUGAR
2 EGG WHITES
1 TBSPN LEMON JUICE

Soften gelatine in water. Crush one cup of blueberries and bring to the boil in a saucepan. Add sugar and gelatine and stir until the gelatine has dissolved. Cool until partially thickened. Beat the egg whites until they peak and then add with lemon juice to the mixture. Stir in the remaining cup of fresh blueberries and allow to set.

Blueberry Buckle

In European ski resorts blueberries are made into soup as a cold cure. In the United States they do the same thing as a cure for diarrhoea. I've never made blueberry soup. This delicious dessert recipe, gleaned from my favourite blueberry grower, seems to keep everyone healthy and happy.

CAKE:
1 TSPN LEMON JUICE
1/3 CUP MILK
60 G MARGARINE
3/4 CUP SUGAR
1 EGG
2 TSPN GRATED LEMON RIND
1 1/2 CUPS PLAIN FLOUR
2 TSPN BAKING POWDER
PINCH OF SALT
2 CUPS BLUEBERRIES,
   FRESH OR FROZEN

Stir lemon juice into milk and set aside. Beat margarine, sugar, egg and lemon rind to a smooth paste and add lemon juice/milk mixture. Mix in dry ingredients to form a smooth batter and then gently add blueberries. Bake in a 20 cm square tin in a 180°C oven for 40–45 minutes, or until the centre is firm and springy to touch.

GLAZE:
2 TBSPN SOFT MARGARINE
1/4 CUP SUGAR
1 TBSPN LEMON JUICE

While cake is cooking, combine glaze ingredients and cook over a low heat until smooth. When the cake is done, spread the glaze over the top and then return it to the oven until the glaze bubbles. Serve cut into small squares, and enjoy the accolades.

Whatever life
serves up . . .

one does accept

. . . one can't always

have their cake
and eat it too!

Kiwi and Almond Slice

One of the reasons kiwi fruit first hit the bargain tables was that people didn't know what else to do with them except eat them fresh and garnish plates with them. That's when I got a kiwi obsession and cooked kiwi dishes till the boys thought I was possessed.

My kiwi challenge was relentless. Despite the boys groaning as they saw me unloading yet another huge bag of two-dollars-a-kilo fruit into the kitchen table fruit baskets, there were nothing but pleasurable responses to the resulting dessert delights.

BASE:
1 1/4 CUPS PLAIN FLOUR
1/4 CUP SUGAR
1 1/4 TSPN BAKING POWDER
PINCH OF SALT
4 TBSPN BUTTER
3 TBSPN MILK
1 EGG
1 TSPN VANILLA
2 CUPS PEELED AND SLICED
    KIWIS

Combine dry ingredients and rub in butter to achieve a coarse breadcrumb consistency. Combine milk, egg and vanilla and mix in well. Spread the mixture in a greased, lined 20–25 cm square baking pan. Place the sliced kiwi fruit evenly over the top.

TOPPING:
3/4 CUP PLAIN FLOUR
1/2 CUP SOFT BROWN SUGAR
1/4 TSPN CINNAMON
4 TBSPN BUTTER
1/2 CUP FLAKED ALMONDS

Place flour, sugar and cinnamon in a bowl. Rub in butter until it has a rough, crumbly consistency. Incorporate almonds and spread over the kiwi fruit. Bake in a 190°C oven for 45 minutes, or until golden. Serve warm, or cold with cream.

Kiwi Fool

The other name for kiwi fruit is Chinese gooseberry. The kiwi has much of the flavour and character of the gooseberry. Which is why I sought out various old English gooseberry recipes and adapted them to kiwi. This is one of them.

1 CUP SUGAR
1 CUP WATER
2 CUPS PEELED AND COARSELY
    CHOPPED KIWI
1 CUP WHIPPED CREAM

Dissolve the sugar in the water and bring it to the boil. Add the kiwis, stirring in well over the heat and then removing the pot so the fruit can cool in the syrup. When cool, drain the syrup and puree the kiwi fruit. Combine the kiwi fruit with the whipped cream and place in serving bowls, garnished with slivers of fresh kiwi. Serve chilled.

she drew her own conclusions ...

Kiwi Crunch

This recipe was inspired by the back of an oatmeal box. It's a health food version of a crumble – very hearty with the added advantage of oats' nutritive properties: protein, iron, zinc, potassium, manganese and Vitamin E. Not that I'd dare to tell the boys a dessert was good for them!

2 CUPS KIWI AND SYRUP, AS IN
   THE PREVIOUS RECIPE
2 TBSPN SAGO
1¼ CUPS OATMEAL
1¼ CUPS RAW SUGAR
2 TBSPN MARGARINE

Place the kiwis and syrup in a greased baking dish (about 22 cm in diameter) and sprinkle evenly with sago. Mix the remaining ingredients in a separate bowl, rubbing to amalgamate into a crumble texture. Spread this about over the top of the kiwi and sago and pop in the middle of a 180°C oven for about 40 minutes until top is brown and crispy. Allow to cool a little before serving with cream or ice cream.

Kiwi Brulee

This also worked with gooseberries, so I tried it with kiwis. Forget the gooseberries. This is better.

8 KIWI FRUIT, PEELED, HALVED
   LENGTHWISE AND SLICED
500 ML CREAM, WHIPPED FIRM
SOFT BROWN SUGAR
   AS REQUIRED

Place the kiwis so they fill two-thirds of an ovenproof dish. Spread the whipped cream over the top and refrigerate for about half an hour. Then cover the cream with a 1 cm layer of soft brown sugar. Chill again for half an hour or so, then pop the whole thing under the griller until the cream bubbles up and the sugar melts into it, creating a toffee-like crust on top. Serve immediately.

Kiwi Pudding

It's often said that men will only eat fruit if it is cut up for them. I know this to be true – which is why I keep finding new and wonderful ways to cut and serve the cheapest fruit of the season. My boys will eat kiwis cooked this way until they can gorge no more. Be warned. It's moreish.

8 KIWI FRUIT, PEELED AND DICED
1 1/2 TBSPN SOFT BROWN SUGAR
2 TSPN GROUND GINGER
90 G MARGARINE
1/3 CUP CASTER SUGAR
1 EGG
1 CUP SELF-RAISING FLOUR
DRIZZLE OF MILK

Place the kiwi fruit in a greased ovenproof dish and sprinkle with brown sugar and half the ginger. Beat the margarine and sugar, adding egg, flour, the remaining ginger and a little milk to spoonable consistency. Spoon mixture over the kiwi fruit and bake in a 180°C oven for 45 minutes until the top browns. Serve hot with cream.

Kiwi Cake

This recipe is adapted from a traditional German cake.

BASE:
1/2 CUP CASTER SUGAR
100 G BUTTER
2 EGGS
1 HEAPED CUP
   SELF-RAISING FLOUR
PINCH OF SALT
1 TSPN VANILLA ESSENCE
DRIZZLE OF MILK

Grease and line a 20–25 cm round deep cake tin, preferably of the springform variety. Make the base by beating sugar and butter to a light cream and adding the eggs and a teaspoon of flour. Beat well, then add flour, salt, vanilla and a little milk to give a smooth (but not pouring) cake consistency.

TOPPING:
8 KIWI FRUIT, PEELED
   AND CHOPPED
2/3 CUP SELF-RAISING FLOUR
1/3 CUP CASTER SUGAR
75 G BUTTER, SLICED
1 TBSPN WATER
ICING SUGAR AS REQUIRED

Spread the base in the bottom of the tin and cover with kiwi fruit pieces. Place flour, sugar and sliced butter in a bowl and work with fingers until finely blended. Add water to give light, lumpy texture. Sprinkle over the kiwis. Bake for about an hour in the centre of a 180°C oven until brown. Cool cake in tin before dusting with icing sugar.

Orange Fluff

Son carried the crumbling old page of newsprint into the kitchen and presented it to me like some sort of prize. Helping a rural friend to clear out a shed, he had found a 1916 country paper with some 'very mum' recipes on it. This was one of them, which was cooked up ceremoniously and consumed with intense curiosity about ancestral lifestyles and general observations that 'olden days food was pretty good, eh?' This is probably the only archaic recipe for which I have a boy to thank.

1^1/$_2$ SACHETS/15 G POWDERED
   GELATINE
^{1}/$_4$ CUP COLD WATER
3 EGGS
^{1}/$_3$ CUP WHITE SUGAR
JUICE OF 2 ORANGES
JUICE OF ^{1}/$_2$ LEMON

Sprinkle the gelatine onto the water in a little saucepan and allow to absorb for a few minutes. Then give it some gentle heat and a stir to dissolve the gelatine. Set it aside and separate the eggs. In one bowl, give the yolks a furious whisking with half the sugar and then, still whisking, add the juice of the oranges and lemons and then the gelatine. Stand the mixture to rest for a while. When it looks like it is starting to set, whisk it a bit more. That's the cue to whip up the egg whites. Whip them to peaks and then add the remaining sugar so that they cream a bit. Fold and stir the fluffy whites into the orange/eggy mixture, making sure to reach the bottom of the bowl so everything is well blended. Put the lot in the fridge and leave it to set for an hour.

Passionfruit Flummery

If you've ever had a passion vine, you've had a glut. This is a glut special. An excellent old-fashioned solution to nature's excess.

1 TBSPN GELATINE
1/2 CUP COLD WATER
1/2 CUP ORANGE JUICE
1 CUP SUGAR
2 TBSPN PLAIN FLOUR
1 CUP HOT WATER
10 PASSIONFRUIT
JUICE OF 1 LEMON

Soak the gelatine in the cold water. In a saucepan, make a smooth paste with some of the orange juice and the sugar and flour, adding the remaining orange juice, then the hot water before stirring over a medium heat until the mixture thickens. Remove from heat and dissolve gelatine in the hot mixture. Cool, then chill the mixture. Once it is nice and thick, beat it furiously into a firm froth. Press the juice from half the passionfruit pulp through a sieve into the mixture and toss in the other half, seeds and all. Add lemon juice. Give the mixture another thorough beating and pour into a bowl to set in the fridge. Forget the cream or ice cream—it's scrumptious as it is.

Poached Pears

When a lad goes to the trouble of writing down a recipe, does it mean he's thinking about leaving home?

I was living under the assumption that our domestic status quo would never change. For years boys had been gathering at the House of the Raising Sons in what seemed to be an exponential exercise in fellowship.

Suddenly, the older boy population became more fluid. And they started to ask serious questions about how things had been cooked and whether I would mind if they wrote down the recipes. Not so much the writing on the wall as in the personal cookbook, I think. The boys were on the move into the big, wide world.

The first time I cooked this recipe, I introduced it to a number of lads who had not encountered it. Their rhapsody was most rewarding. And I was deeply touched when two of them, separately and secretly, sought me out to ask for the recipe. It is a delicious dish that we should all make the most of every year when pears are in autumn abundance. The recipe can take variations according to taste.

1 CUP WATER
1 CUP RED WINE
1 TSPN LEMON JUICE
1 CUP SUGAR
1 STICK OF CINNAMON
6 SWEET EATING PEARS,
   PEELED BUT NOT CORED
3 TSPN ARROWROOT

Heat the water, wine, lemon juice and sugar in a saucepan until the sugar is dissolved, add the cinnamon stick and then place the pears (preferably standing) in the hot juice and cover with a lid. Simmer gently for half an hour until the pears are a pinkish colour. Remove the pears and the cinnamon stick from the syrup. Blend the arrowroot to a runny paste with a little water and carefully add it to the pear syrup, stirring. Bring to the boil, then stir for a few minutes until the syrup is clear. The syrup will thicken as it cools. Spoon it over the pears and chill. Serve with whipped cream.

Pear Casserole

Peaceful contentment falls over the House of the Raising Sons. The hungry horde is sated once again. Another long day is almost over. These late quiet times of the night are mums' times. We pad softly through the house checking on sleeping forms, picking up strewn unspeakables, switching off blithely burning lights and locking up.

The world is serene. There's no throbbing rap music from the young teen scene and no melancholy guitar with experimental harmonies from the older lads. Only the monotone hum of the computer, reminding me that it is old and faithful.

I ponder how many trillions of mothers may be in the same private nocturnal mode – reflecting on the day's events, on the problems of the children, on the bills, on the oncoming day's necessities and on how the food may be stretched through the week. There's comfort in the universality of our role.

But, as with all things in the maternal mode, such thoughts must be swift. First things first. Food.

To capitalise on my often bountiful supply of pears when they are in season, I use one of the simplest and cheapest recipes in history. This has been an ecstatic triumph with my teen tribe.

6 PEARS
6 SLICES WHITE BREAD
BUTTER AS REQUIRED
BROWN SUGAR AS REQUIRED
CINNAMON AS REQUIRED
6 CLOVES
6 TBSPN SHERRY, PORT OR BOTH

Peel and core pears. Remove crusts and then butter bread on both sides and line the base of a casserole with the pieces – about two slices deep. Sprinkle generously with soft brown sugar and powdered cinnamon. Place the pears on top and stick a clove in each one. Pour a tablespoon of sherry, port or a mixture of both over each pear. Cover and bake in a 180°C oven until the pears are soft. This will take about an hour. Serve with cream or custard.

Pears with Coffee and Honey Sauce

Pears poach wonderfully in almost anything from wine to tangelo juice. Coffee is no exception.

6 RIPE, FIRM PEARS, PEELED
    AND CORED
2 TBSPN LEMON JUICE
1 CUP STRONG, HOT
    BLACK COFFEE
1/2 CUP HONEY
300 ML WHIPPED CREAM
GRATED CHOCOLATE FOR
    DECORATION (OPTIONAL)

Brush pears with lemon juice to keep their colour and pack in a heavy-based saucepan. Combine hot coffee with honey, pour over pears and poach, covered, until the pears are cooked, about 20 minutes. Remove the pears. Boil syrup for about 15 minutes to thicken and then pour over the pears. When cool, chill and then serve with whipped cream and chocolate.

Mango Bliss

Since mangoes became affordable and available almost all year round, the actual mango season has turned into a bounty – sometimes to the point that one realises with embarrassment that one had better do some prompt mango-consuming or they'll go nasty in the fruit bowl. That's the time for Mango Bliss, another variation on the light and fluffy desserts which cost so little and make everyone so utterly contented – not to mention dosed up with fruity vitamins.

3/4 CUP FRESH ORANGE JUICE
2 1/2 TSPN PLAIN POWDERED
    GELATINE
1 1/2 CUPS PUREED FRESH MANGO
    FLESH
2 EGG WHITES
2 TBSPN SUGAR
1 1/2 TSPN PURE VANILLA
1/4 TSPN SALT

Warm the orange juice and stir in the gelatine until it is well dissolved. Add the mango puree. Mix well and cool until it is just starting to firm up. Then, whip the egg whites to frothy soft peaks, adding the sugar, vanilla and salt, and carefully and evenly fold it into the mango. Pour into fancy serving glasses or leave it in the bowl and chill for about eight hours. Serve with a dollop of cream.

Spanish Crumble

Bargain cooking apples are always a good find. There are no end of things to do with apples. In a quest for something completely different, I took the teen tribe travelling to flavours they might encounter in a Spanish kitchen.

Their enchantment evidenced itself in a fairly disgusting display of greed. This Iberian variation on apple crumble is better than our own.

1 KG COOKING APPLES
(GRANNIES)
3 LEVEL TSPN DRIED
MINT LEAVES
3 LEVEL TSPN CINNAMON
BUTTER AS REQUIRED
1 CUP WHITE SUGAR
$1/4$ TSPN BAKING POWDER
$2/3$ CUP PLAIN FLOUR
1 EGG

Peel, core and cut the apples into 5 mm slices, then toss them thoroughly in mixed mint and cinnamon before packing them into the bottom of a well-buttered 20 cm baking tray. In a bowl blend the remaining dry ingredients before adding the egg and mixing it evenly to achieve a heavy crumbly consistency. Spread this over the apples and press it down well. Cook in a 180°C oven for about an hour. The top should be quite firm and crisp. Cover and allow to cool and settle before slicing. Serve with whipped cream.

Spanish Cream

Another of those sublime old dishes which seems to have faded from the world. This is the 'proper' way to do it. It's worth that little bit of extra effort for the richer flavour.

2 TSPN/10 G SACHET GELATINE
2 CUPS MILK
3 EGGS
2 TBSPN SUGAR
FEW DROPS OF VANILLA
  OR ROSE ESSENCE

Soak gelatine in milk for 20–30 minutes. Beat egg yolks and whites separately. Rinse a bowl or mould with cold water. Warm the milk and gelatine gently. Do not boil. Add beaten egg yolks and sugar and stir vigorously. Cook over a gentle heat, stirring, until the mixture begins to thicken. Remove from heat and stir in the essence and firmly beaten egg whites before pouring into the bowl to cool and set. This is very nice served with stewed fruit.

Cindy's American Pumpkin Pie

The *pièce de résistance* is American-style pumpkin pie. I couldn't imagine what all the fuss was about until a young American exchange student gave me this apparently classic American recipe years ago. It is sheer, custardy bliss.

3 EGGS
2 CUPS COOKED AND PUREED
    PUMPKIN
1 CUP SOFT BROWN SUGAR
PINCH OF SALT
1 TSPN GINGER
1 TSPN CINNAMON
1/4 TSPN POWDERED CLOVES
1 TSPN NUTMEG
300 ML EVAPORATED MILK
SHORTCRUST PASTRY SHELL,
    UNCOOKED, IN A LARGE ROUND
    PYREX OR CAKE TIN AT LEAST
    22 CM IN DIAMETER

Heat the oven to 230°C. Beat the eggs in a large bowl, then beat in pumpkin and other ingredients. Ladle into the pastry and place in the centre of the oven for 15 minutes. Turn the heat down to 150°C for 40 more minutes, until the filling seems set. Cool on a wire rack.

Ovenly Pancake

On the economy of effort front, I've discovered a brilliant European alternative to the labour-intensive business of pancake making. You simply cook the pancake mix in one hit, then slice it and serve with jam and cream.

It sounds odd, it looks quaint, but it turns out to be a delicious, easy and gloriously inexpensive dessert which is so belly-filling that it can perform the miracle of bringing, for a while at least, a serene soporific silence to the usually rowdy House of the Raising Sons.

2 EGGS
2¹/₂ CUPS MILK
1 TBSPN SUGAR
PINCH OF SALT
FEW DROPS VANILLA ESSENCE
1¹/₂ CUPS PLAIN FLOUR

Beat the eggs into half the milk with the sugar, salt and vanilla essence, then trickle in the flour until it makes an even batter. Slowly add the rest of the milk. Beat well. Allow to stand for 15 minutes and then pour into a well-greased medium-sized pyrex baking dish – about 25 cm in diameter. Bake at about 210°C for 30–40 minutes, until the top is golden brown. Serve with jam and whipped cream or ice cream.

Golden Pud

Golden pud goes by many names. It's one of those classic, el-cheapo wintry treats that are in the repertoire of any family cook who has so much as a drop of English blood in their veins.

175 G BUTTER
3/4 CUP SUGAR
3 EGGS (SEPARATED)
1 TBSPN MILK
1 1/4 CUPS SELF-RAISING FLOUR
BUTTER AS REQUIRED
1/4 CUP GOLDEN SYRUP
JUICE OF 1 LEMON

Cream butter and sugar until light. Beat in the three egg yolks, milk and flour to make a stiff dough. Separately beat the egg whites until they begin to peak. Fold the egg whites into the dough. Meanwhile, prepare a pudding basin by rubbing it generously with butter and pouring the golden syrup and lemon juice into the bottom. Place the dough on top of this and then cover well. I use one layer of greaseproof paper and then wrap the whole thing in foil. Place the basin in a steamer, cover with lid and steam for two hours. Then invert the pudding onto a deep serving dish so all the sweet juices run down the sides. Served hot with lashings of cream.

There are many variations on this sponge-pudding theme. You can turn it into a:

- Jam Sponge Pudding – by replacing the syrup and lemon with about five tablespoons of any favourite jam.
- Lemon Pudding – by adding the finely-grated rind of a lemon to the pudding mixture.
- Apricot Pudding – by putting a layer of stewed and pureed apricots on the bottom.
- Almond Pudding – by replacing a tablespoon of flour with a tablespoon of ground almonds and a few drops of almond essence.

Chocolate Stodge Pud

I pride myself in being an humanitarian mum. On occasions I will indulge the boys in stodge, because every boy loves stodge. Almost as much as I do.

60 G BUTTER
1/2 CUP MILK
1 TSPN VANILLA ESSENCE
1 CUP SELF-RAISING FLOUR
3/4 CUP CASTER SUGAR
1 TBSPN COCOA

TOPPING:
3/4 CUP BROWN SUGAR
1 TBSPN COCOA
2 CUPS HOT WATER

Melt butter by warming with milk. Add vanilla essence and pour into the combined dry ingredients, beating until smooth. Place this mixture in a greased two-liter ovenproof dish, then sprinkle the dry topping ingredients over the batter and, very carefully, pour the hot water on top. Put immediately into a 180°C oven and bake in the middle for 45 minutes, by which time the pudding will have risen to the top and a rich chocolate sauce will be bubbling beneath and around the sides. Serve warm with fresh cream.

Sweet Afterthoughts

··

What's the difference between spring and teenagers? One's weather a lot and the other's whether or not. Essentially, though, they have a great deal in common since neither seems to know exactly what it wants to be. They can both be things of great joy and of immense frustration.

When spring returns the weather to storms, slush and wet washing, the teenagers are on school holidays and are, more often than not, wreaking havoc in my house and with my stress levels.

When the youthful hordes are not moving house to house as a massive eating entity, they're networking extravagantly by phone to orchestrate these mass movements.

How to cater for their variable and unpredictable numbers? I haven't time to set up party smorgasbords overnight and one must presume that at least some of them have homes where occasionally they can drop in for a feed.

So I turn out sweet snack food which is quick, easy and cheap.

Muffins

Boy, have I trotted batches of hot muffins out of my kitchen. Plain muffins with butter, or butter and jam. Banana muffins. Banana and pineapple muffins. Apricot muffins. Cheese muffins. Cherry muffins. And, favourite of all, blueberry muffins made from lovely, plump frozen berries.

Nobody seems to tire of muffins – and there are dozens of variations to experiment with. The trick with muffins is not to overmix them or let the mixture lie around for long before cooking. Make sure the oven is hot – 200°C – and pop them straight in.

This is the classic American formula:

(TO MAKE A DOZEN MUFFINS)
1 EGG
1 CUP MILK
3 TBSPN MELTED BUTTER
  OR MARGARINE
2 CUPS PLAIN FLOUR
3 HEAPED TSPN BAKING POWDER
PINCH OF SALT
1/3 CUP SUGAR

Combine wet ingredients and add quickly to the well-blended dry ingredients. Do not beat. Pour batter into greased muffin tins, filling two-thirds. Bake immediately in a 200°C oven for 20–25 minutes until golden brown.

For variation, I like to substitute two-thirds of a cup of yoghurt and one-third of a cup of milk for the one cup of milk in the recipe.

To have varied flavours of muffins, add one cup of the chosen fruit to this mixture. This can be finely chopped apple (with a little cinnamon), sultanas, currants, chopped prunes, drained crushed pineapple and/or mashed bananas. In the case of blueberries or tinned stoned cherries, let the muffins rest in the tins for a while before putting them on a wire rack. Otherwise they will break up with the weight of the hot fruit.

For cheese muffins, add half a cup of grated cheese.

For parsley muffins, which are good with soups, omit the sugar and add two tablespoons of chopped parsley. The same applies to chives or mixed herbs.

For bran muffins, substitute one cup of bran for one of the cups of plain flour.

Muffin variations are limited only by what's at hand in the kitchen.

American Blueberry Biscuits

A cookie and a glass of milk? What sort of request is that from a strapping Aussie lad? *Brady Bunch* subliminals? Has the Great Cultural Imperialism struck at the core of our domestic snack conditioning?

Whatever happened to a Vegemite sandwich and a cup of tea? Or lemonade and a bickie?

The boys of the House of the Raising Sons, in line with just about every other kid in the state, wear baseball caps of teams they've never seen, 'sneakers' instead of sandshoes and think Hersheys have something over Cadburys.

I was satisfying the lads very well with a fit of cultural indignation over the 'partly teasing' cookie provocation. They know what buttons to press on a mum, these lads. When things are looking a bit dull around the house, stirring up mum is good sport.

I decided I would not give them the satisfaction. But I would not surrender. 'The word,' I told them, 'is biscuit. And biscuits you shall have.'

With that, I foraged through the American cookbooks to satisfy something which, truth be told, has gnawed at my curiosity for years – just what do the Americans think a biscuit is?

Well, it's a sort of a savoury scone. They like to have them with gravy on main meals. Maybe it's in lieu of bread rolls. Since the household was not in a savoury mood, I found a compromise 'biscuit' combination and, playing with it just a bit to suit the Aussie palate, turned out a batch of the most sensational afternoon snacks. They're not sweet and they're not savoury. They are a whole new taste sensation, and they finally have the boys asking for 'biscuits'.

1/4 CUP MARGARINE
2 CUPS PLAIN FLOUR
1 TBSPN BAKING POWDER
PINCH OF SALT
1 CUP MILK
1 1/2 CUPS FRESH BLUEBERRIES
SPRINKLE OF SUGAR

Cut the margarine into the dry ingredients in a bowl, working with your fingers until the mixture is crumbly, and then add the milk until well mixed but not beaten. Incorporate blueberries and drop spoonfuls of the batter onto a greased baking sheet. Sprinkle the tops liberally with sugar, and bake for 12–15 minutes in a 230°C oven.

Banana-Apricot Loaf

Dried apricots give a lovely tang to all sorts of things. They certainly give a lift to a banana loaf.

1 1/4 CUPS PLAIN FLOUR
2/3 CUP SUGAR
2 TSPN BAKING POWDER
PINCH OF SALT
1/2 TSPN BAKING SODA
1/2 CUP MARGARINE
1 CUP MASHED BANANAS
1 CUP FINELY CHOPPED
   DRIED APRICOTS
2 EGGS, SLIGHTLY BEATEN

Mix the dry ingredients in a bowl, then work in the margarine with your fingers until the mix is crumbly. Stir in the bananas, apricots and eggs until evenly blended. Then spread the batter in a greased and floured loaf tin (approximately 23 x 13 cm) and bake for an hour in the middle of a 180°C oven. Check with a skewer to see whether it is cooked in the centre. If the skewer comes from the centre dry and the edges of the loaf have parted from the tin, then it should be perfect. Cool on a wire rack for 10 minutes before removing from the tin.

Quick Coconut Cake

This was the very first cake I made and it has remained a steadfast favourite as an ideal 'quickie' to knock up when there's need of cake in the house.

250 G MARGARINE, MELTED
1½ CUPS SUGAR
2 CUPS SELF-RAISING FLOUR
2 CUPS COCONUT
3 EGGS
1 CUP MILK

Melt the margarine in a large saucepan. Stir in the sugar and allow to cool slightly, then add all the other ingredients. Put into a well-greased and lined tin and bake at 180°C for 40 minutes.

Mum's Orange Nut Loaf

This is one of the nicest nut loaves in the business. I kept baking it with the plan of putting it in school lunches – but it never lasted long enough to get there.

2¾ CUPS PLAIN FLOUR
1 CUP SUGAR
PINCH OF SALT
1 TSPN BAKING POWDER
1 TSPN BAKING SODA
6 TBSPN CHOPPED NUTS
   (PREFERABLY ALMONDS)
2 ORANGES (RIND AND JUICE)
WATER AS REQUIRED
2 TBSPN MELTED MARGARINE
1 EGG, SLIGHTLY BEATEN
1 TSPN VANILLA

Mix dry ingredients in a bowl. Lightly grate the zest (the oily exterior skin of the orange), avoiding the white pith. Squeeze out the juice and add to it enough water to make just under one-and-a-half cups (284 ml, the old half pint, is what I use). Mix together all the wet ingredients, including the grated rind, then pour them into the dry ingredients and blend thoroughly. Place in a lined, medium-sized loaf tin and bake for an hour at 180°C. Turn onto a wire rack to cool.

Yummies

My mother, a superb cook, always claimed that her culinary secret was that everything was 'cooked with love'. Perhaps love is the special ingredient in home-baked bikkies. Certainly they are always enthusiastically greeted by my snack-happy clan.

So fast are they wolfed down that one really must do something of a production-line job to make them last. That's why Yummies are a favourite recipe.

They can be given almost infinite variety, not to mention entertainment value in the making, with the assorted additions. The base recipe is, so to speak, a piece of cake.

(TO MAKE APPROXIMATELY TWENTY BISCUITS)
3/4 CUP CASTER SUGAR
175 G MARGARINE
1 EGG
2 CUPS SELF-RAISING FLOUR

Cream the sugar and margarine before adding the egg and then the flour. Rest the dough for 15 minutes in the fridge while assembling goodies such as:

CORNFLAKES
COCONUT
GLACE CHERRIES
SULTANAS
RICE CRISPIES
COCOA
BROWN SUGAR
GLACE PEEL
HUNDREDS AND THOUSANDS

Then portion off the dough into smallish balls, flatten slightly and roll in or press on the chosen additions to give a wide variety of versions. Bake on a greased tray for 10–12 minutes at 180°C.

Oats Crunchies

Biscuits can also be health foods. Now that oats are known to be so stunningly good for you, these old-fashioned oats crunchies are just the ticket for the ticker and the intestinal system. By sweet chance, they're also positively delectable.

225 G BUTTER OR MARGARINE
2¼ CUPS PORRIDGE OATS
½ CUP WHEAT GERM FLAKES
  (OR EXTRA OATS)
¾ CUP RAW SUGAR

Melt the margarine. Combine the oats, wheat germ and sugar and then blend in the melted margarine. Press the lot into a greased swiss roll tin and bake at 190°C for 10–15 minutes until golden brown. Cool before slicing.

Golden Crispies

Come the inevitable school fete, there must be at least one quick, easy, cheap, biscuit-style recipe which neither demolishes the kitchen nor takes all of the night before. This is it, guaranteed to appeal to all feteophiles.

4 TBSPN GOLDEN SYRUP
1 TBSPN SUGAR
1 TBSPN MARGARINE
FEW DROPS OF VANILLA ESSENCE
2½ CUPS RICE CRISPIES

Bring the syrup, sugar and margarine to the boil in a saucepan. Boil for one minute. Add vanilla essence. Cool for five minutes and then add rice crispies. Mix well and pack into a greased 20 cm square tin. Cool, cut and store in the fridge.

Idiot Biscuits

Any fool can make these.

115 G BUTTER
1/4 CUP SUGAR
1 TSPN VANILLA ESSENCE
3/4 CUP PLAIN FLOUR
1 TBSPN COCOA POWDER

Cream butter and sugar, and add vanilla. Mix in flour and cocoa, handworking it into a firm dough. Break off smallish sections, roll into balls and place on a greased baking sheet. Flatten them with the back of a fork and bake in a 180°C oven for 20–30 minutes.

Ginger Bickies

Ever since I found out that ginger is an antioxidant, I've been calling these a healthfood.

85 G MARGARINE
1 TBSPN GOLDEN SYRUP
1 1/4 CUPS SELF-RAISING FLOUR
1/3 CUP CASTER SUGAR
2 LEVEL TSPN GINGER

Melt margarine and syrup. Cool before blending thoroughly into the dry ingredients. Place teaspoons of the mixture on an ungreased baking tray and cook in the lower middle of a 200°C oven for 12–15 minutes.

Sour Cream Chocolate Cake

Children are terrifying markers of the fast-flying years. Suddenly, the baby one carried so easily on the hip is a young man smiling down from some great height. One feels no older but is mercilessly reminded by all this relentless growing. Ah, the melancholy of losing little ones to opinionated semi-adulthood.

Another birthday rolls around and as the birthday boy counts his presents, mother reflects on giving birth all those years ago and why on earth kids don't give mums presents for having them in the first place. Instead, of course, the kids' birthdays represent another burst of hard work.

I can't remember when I first began making this birthday cake. It has become a ritual institution cooked only at birthdays to keep its treat value. But in truth it is one of the best of easy chocolate cakes and could get more mileage in houses of frequent cake-eaters.

2 CUPS PLAIN FLOUR
1 CUP WATER
3/4 CUP SOUR CREAM
   OR YOGHURT
1 TSPN VANILLA
2 EGGS
2 CUPS SUGAR
1/4 CUP COOKING MARGARINE
1 1/2 TSPN BAKING SODA
PINCH OF SALT
1/2 TSPN BAKING POWDER
12 TBSPN COCOA

With the oven preheated to 180°C, grease and flour three layer pans. Put all the ingredients in a mixing bowl and beat from slow to fast until smooth, about four minutes. Pour into the three tins and bake for 25 minutes. Join the layers with good jam. Apricot is delicious. Top with lots of chocolate butter icing (butter or soft margarine, icing sugar and cocoa). For complete excess, serve with whipped cream and strawberry garnish.

Coconut and Jam Fingers

Sometimes I make too much jam. Sometimes there are jams which, mysteriously, just can't get themselves eaten. These are the raisons d'etre of this delicious snack. You can spread different jams on different parts of the pastry. You can spread them thick or you can spread them thin. I like it thick and usually use the best part of a jar of jam.

110 G MARGARINE
1/2 CUP CASTER SUGAR
1 EGG
FEW DROPS OF VANILLA ESSENCE
1 1/2 CUPS PLAIN FLOUR
JAM AS REQUIRED

TOPPING:
1 EGG
1/2 CUP CASTER SUGAR
1 CUP DESICCATED COCONUT

Cream the margarine and sugar until light. Add the egg and vanilla, then stir in the flour. This makes a dough mixture which should then be spread and carefully pressed down into a well-greased and floured swiss roll tin. Cover the dough layer with jam in liberal quantities. Mix the egg and sugar together and add the coconut. This makes a crumbly topping. Sprinkle it evenly over the top of the jam. Bake in a 180°C oven for 25–30 minutes. Cut into fingers while still hot.

Marmalade Cake

The King may have liked marmalade instead in the old nursery rhyme but the boys, well, they never were too keen on marmalade, not even my superb kumquat version. And there's that thing about marmalade. More people make it than like it. It is the great surplus crop of all preserves. People are constantly giving it away. Giving it to me, as it happens.

I was surreptitiously throwing it away until I discovered that the clever old Scots had a few alternative things one could do with it, things that the boys really liked, as it turned out. And suddenly, not only was the glut over, but I was glad of every new jar of marmalade.

3 EGGS
6 OZ BUTTER
6 OZ CASTER SUGAR
10 OZ SR FLOUR
FINELY GRATED ZEST OF A LARGE
   ORANGE
1 HEAPED TBSPN CHOPPED
   MIXED PEEL
3 TBSPN MARMALADE
   (WITH TEXTURE, NOT THE
   BLENDER SORT)
1/2 CUP FRESH ORANGE JUICE

MAKE ICING WITH 1/3 CUP ICING
   SUGAR AND 2 TBSPN ORANGE
   JUICE

Grease and line an 18–20 cm round cake pan. Separate the eggs. Cream butter and sugar, adding a tablespoon of flour and then beating the egg yolks in gradually. On very slow beat, add zest, mixed peel and marmalade and lastly the flour. Beat the egg whites until they can hold a soft mound and then carefully fold them into the cake mix. Tip into cake pan and bake in the centre of a 180°C (350°F) oven for about an hour, until the cake is golden brown on top and firm to the touch. Cool for 10 mins before turning out on a wire rack. When cold, mix the icing sugar and orange juice so it can lift like firm butter on the side of a knife and, thus, cover the top of the cake. If it runs down the side a bit, fine.

Forget the Fizz

. . . .

The sight of families rolling up to the supermarket checkout with trolleys groaning full of fizzy soda drinks always gives me the budgetary shudders. How do they afford it? Are they screamingly rich or are they just terribly impractical with their money?

At the rate my growing action pack guzzles drinks, I can't afford to fill the fridge with bottled lollywaters. For us the odd Woodies, Coke or Pepsi has to be a holiday treat.

I use several fresh fruit cordial recipes to keep young thirsts cheaply and nutritionally quenched. But I'm admitting that, despite a lifelong devotion to Bickfords lime juice, I'm not much of a one for sugary drinks.

Come the fluid depletions of steamy summer, I find nothing more refreshing, sustaining, delicious and, most importantly, economical than iced tea.

In hot weather I keep at least two jugs of iced tea and one jug of chilled mint and lemon water in the fridge. Apart from restoring the fluid balance, these old-fashioned home-made drinks are a darned sight healthier than anything one can buy.

Harriced Tea

The world of tea drinkers is no longer a dull place. For special and varied taste sensations, I choose from among the tea exotica available at the markets – tropical star tea, vanilla, rose petal, bilberry . . . the range is huge and, since you need only small quantities, it's not a budget-breaking investment.

I also frequent the Asian supermarkets where I can buy wonderful ready-mixed ginger teas, angelica root tea, honeysuckle tea and that strange, sweet fruit tea called Lo-Han-Kuo. But Liptons will do just fine.

If you have rainwater, it makes by far the finest tea. And don't forget the old rules about warming the pot and bringing the pot to the kettle.

4 TSPN CHOSEN TEA
  (ROSE PETAL FOR ME)
1 ROSEHIP TEABAG
A THUMB OF FRESH GINGER,
  SLICED
1 LEMON, 1/2 JUICED AND
  1/2 SLICED
SUGAR TO TASTE
WATER AS REQUIRED

Brew tea with rosehip teabag in the usual manner. Place other ingredients in the bottom of a large jug, add a cup of cold water, then strain in the full pot of tea. Top up with water. Leave to cool and then refrigerate. Serve with or without ice.

Lemon Mint Water

Squeeze the juice of one lemon into a jug of water and add a couple of sprigs of well-washed fresh mint, slightly crushed. Leave in the fridge to infuse, and drink chilled. Sweet-tooths can add sugar.

Lassi

Iced tea has long been popular in tropical Asia as a stimulant and a refresher. And it's from Asia that this wonderful summer sustainer comes. The Indians often accompany their spicy meals with lassi drinks. Because lassi is a yoghurt-based beverage, it lines and soothes the tummy as well as nourishes and replaces fluids. I sometimes make it by the jug but most often I whip it up by the glass.

1/2 CUP PLAIN YOGHURT
1/2 CUP WATER
2 TSPN SUGAR (OR TO YOUR
    OWN TASTE)
3–4 DROPS ROSEWATER
    (OPTIONAL)

Pour ingredients into a blender and whiz until frothy. Pour into a glass with crushed ice.

Lassi is also made as a savoury drink in which the sugar is replaced by a couple of pinches of salt.

Occasionally I use honey instead of sugar. In fact, once you get going with yoghurt, water and a blender, you are limited only by your imagination and ingredients. Orange juice, fresh peach, passionfruit, mango ... they each incorporate superbly with a yoghurt/water mix and turn the drink into assorted versions of smoothies.

Lemon Squash

Everyone wants this recipe after they have tasted it. Since it contains fresh juice, it does not last forever like a plain sugar cordial. But I've never found its exact shelf life because, no matter how much I make, it vanishes like money in the supermarket.

LEMONS TO YIELD ABOUT
  2¹/₂ CUPS JUICE
1 KG WHITE SUGAR
8 CUPS WATER
2 TSPN CITRIC ACID (OPTIONAL)

Peel the yellow zest from at least half the lemons, making sure not to include the white pith of the skins. Squeeze juice from the fruit and reserve. Place the rind, sugar and water in a stainless steel pan and warm well until the sugar is dissolved and the syrup is a lovely yellow. Strain out the peeled skins, add the fresh lemon juice and citric acid to the syrup and store in clean, sterile bottles.

Orange Cordial

The same drink. Different fruit.

12 FIRM ORANGES
2²/₃ CUPS SUGAR
2¹/₂ CUPS WATER
1 TSPN CITRIC ACID

Wash the oranges and peel most of the oil-bearing orange skin from six oranges with a potato peeler, being careful to avoid the white pith. Place the skin peelings along with the sugar and water into a pan and bring to the boil. Reduce the heat and simmer for 15 minutes. Add the citric acid and allow to cool. Meanwhile, juice all the oranges and add to the syrup. Strain the cordial into sterilised bottles and store.

Lemon Barley Water

Barley water is so easy to make, you will wonder why you haven't been doing it for years. It's one of the few health drinks that does not taste like a health drink.

1 CUP PEARL BARLEY
2 TBSPN SUGAR
WATER AS REQUIRED
FINELY GRATED RIND AND JUICE
    OF 2–3 LEMONS
4 CUPS BOILING WATER

Wash barley, cover with cold water and bring to the boil. Boil for five minutes and strain off the water. Place the barley in a heatproof jug along with the sugar and grated lemon rind. Pour on four cups of boiling water, stir well to dissolve sugar and let cool. Add the lemon juice, strain, chill and drink.

Ginger Cordial

Ginger cordial is a very fresh and pleasant alternative summer drink. We like it with a strong bite of ginger. This is up to individuals, so this version is very mild. Children as young as five love it this way. If you want a strong ginger taste, add more ginger.

6 CUPS WATER
APPROX 10 CM GINGER,
    FINELY SLICED
1 RED CHILI
1/2 TSPN TARTARIC ACID
2 CUPS SUGAR

Place the water, ginger, chili and tartaric acid in a pan and bring to the boil. Stir in the sugar and boil on low bubble for 20–30 minutes. Cool and strain into sterilised bottles. Dilute in the usual way for drinking.

When feeling a little washed out
... a good tap with some unsinkable
chums can leave one positively
gleaming ...

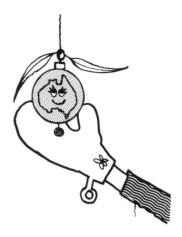

Dreaming of a Tasty Christmas

The relaxing thing about the young generation is its lack of sentiment for the traditional trappings of European Christmas. My teen tribe doesn't give a figgy for pudding. Not even scrupulously sterilised old-currency sixpences whip up enough enthusiasm in them for other than a quick dissection job. Quite sensibly, they find all that long-hung fruit too hot and stodgy for their antipodean summer comfort.

So plum pud is off the menu, dears. And so is the full-catastrophe Christmas fruitcake. Not because we don't like it. My old recipe fruitcake is a brandy-soaked winner but the ingredients alone cost about forty dollars (excluding the booze) and, like so many single-income families, we must respect more pressing financial priorities.

This is not to say we are not going to feast royally throughout Christmas. Budgeting can be beautiful.

Boiled Fruit Cake

One of the cheapest traditional fruit cakes is also the nicest and the easiest. Like most good recipes, one need not adhere rigidly to the listed ingredients. I prefer plump, seedless raisins to currants and use lots of those along with sultanas in this recipe.

2 CUPS DRIED SULTANAS AND
  RAISINS (OR FRUIT OF CHOICE)
1 CUP WATER
1 CUP SOFT BROWN SUGAR
125 G MARGARINE
3 TSPN MIXED SPICE
2 TBSPN BRANDY
2 CUPS PLAIN FLOUR
1 TSPN BICARB OF SODA
1 LARGE EGG

Place the first five ingredients in a stainless steel saucepan, bring to the boil and simmer for about 30 minutes. Allow to cool before adding the brandy and other ingredients. Stir thoroughly and turn into a greased and lined 18–20 cm cake tin. Bake at 180°C for about 90 minutes.

My Aussie Christmas Cake

I love to be a pioneer. That's why I had to invent the new-era Aussie Christmas cake. I think this cake represents the flavour of our climate and diet – rich and light at the same time.

4–5 TBSPN FLAKED ALMONDS
2/3 CUP WHITE SUGAR
150 G SOFT BUTTER
3 EGGS
1 CUP PLAIN FLOUR
1 TSPN BAKING POWDER
PINCH OF SALT
1 CUP CHOPPED DRIED APRICOTS
   (MOIST AND YOUNG)
1/2 CUP CHOPPED PRESERVED
   GINGER
A LITTLE MILK

Pick out a quarter of the best-looking flaked almonds for decoration. Cream the sugar and margarine until light, then beat in the eggs one at a time, adding a teaspoon of flour to prevent them curdling. Mix two tablespoons of flour into the fruit, tossing well. This helps give the fruit even distribution. Add the rest of the dry ingredients, with the fruit last. Drizzle in milk to achieve a semi-stiff dropping consistency. Place the mixture in a greased and lined 18–20 cm cake tin and arrange the reserved almonds decoratively on top. Bake at 180°C for 90 minutes until golden on top and firm to touch.

Poverty Christmas Cake

This is an English shortcut fruit cake. It's one of the best cheat's recipes in the repertoire – and needs not be restricted to Christmas.

75 G MARGARINE
25 G LARD
1/2 CUP SOFT BROWN SUGAR
2 LARGE EGGS
350 G FRUIT MINCEMEAT
  (ONE JAR)
11/3 CUPS SELF-RAISING FLOUR
DRIZZLE OF MILK

Cream fats and sugar, then beat in the eggs. Stir in fruit mince and fold in flour. This should produce a moist mixture. If not, add a little milk. Place the mixture in a greased and lined 18 cm round tin and bake at 180°C for 10 minutes, then turn the oven down to 150°C and cook for 75 minutes, until the top of the cake is firm.

Fruit Petit Four

With our summer fruits so gloriously in season at Christmas, it is absurd not to make a treat of them. Summer pudding is always popular (that classic standard recipe of a white-bread-lined mould filled with strawberries, blueberries and others, which have been warmed with sugar, then sealed with bread and foil, weighted, chilled overnight and turned out). One little yummy that never fails to delight is the petit-four-style of semi-crystallising fresh fruit. It is one of the most civilised accompaniments to a good after-meal coffee.

EGG WHITES AS REQUIRED
CASTER SUGAR AS REQUIRED
STRAWBERRIES, BLUEBERRIES,
  GRAPES AS REQUIRED

Whisk the egg white until it is stiff but not dry. Place caster sugar in a saucer. Dip fruit pieces into the egg white then roll carefully to layer lightly with the sugar. Dry on waxed paper and serve.

All the world is a stage

and life is but
a performance...

for which there is ...

no rehearsal ...

White Christmas

It's our self-sacrificial nature to push ourselves to the extremities to fulfil our young's dreams, not to mention their perilous peer-pressure requirements. That's where Christmas foods become a challenge. One cannot seem to be stinting. One must generate the spirit of plenty and celebration.

So, back to the wisdom of the grannies I go to recall what used to be around to make Christmas wonderful in those lean old post-war days.

White Christmas, of course. A luxurious, easy-to-make and reasonably inexpensive sweetmeat. With a few contemporary adjustments, this old recipe makes quite a festive treat. It scores a 'whoops-it's-all-gone' eleven out of ten from the boys.

2 CUPS RICE BUBBLES
1 CUP COCONUT
1 CUP EQUAL QUANTITIES
   RAISINS, GLACE CHERRIES AND
   GLACE GINGER, CHOPPED
1 CUP POWDERED MILK
   (OR 2/3 CUP HORLICKS)
1 CUP ICING SUGAR
2 TSPN PURE VANILLA ESSENCE
250 G MELTED COPHA
   (COCONUT FAT)

Assemble all the dry ingredients in a mixing bowl, then add the vanilla to the melted copha. Blend well and pour into the fruit mix. Combine everything thoroughly and then press into a lined tin and chill. Cut into squares to serve, and store in an airtight container.

a pair of practical shoes ...

A Tirade of Terrific Tips

The best tip I ever received was to take notice of tips. My wonderful mum told me that, as well as most of the nifty tips I know. She learned most of them from her wonderful mum.

So who really discovers them? And under what dire circumstances of domestic desperation?

For example, who discovered that rhubarb cleans burnt saucepans? And how did they find out? Did they think, 'Well, rhubarb cooks a pan clean, so maybe it cleans an overcooked pan ...', or, 'Gee, that pan is a mess, I think I'll cook some rhubarb in it ...'?

Truth is, rhubarb is not the first thing that springs to mind when I burn a pot. I have never tested the tip, so I have no idea whether or not it works. The following tips, however, are tried and true tricks.

BAKING TRAYS placed under casseroles or pie dishes catch any overflow and save on oven cleaning.

BAMBOO SKEWERS normally used for satays are good for testing if cakes are cooked in the centre.

BEETROOT TOPS should not be wasted. They are an excellent vegetable in themselves and should be washed and cooked as spinach.

BICARBONATE OF SODA in a bowl in the fridge helps to eliminate odours. Bicarb also works as a fire retardent – sprinkle it fast if things under your griller catch fire, or use for a grease fire on the stove.

CHEESE is easier to wash off a grater if you brush the grater with a little oil first.

CHICKEN WINGS are cheap and a good way to make chicken stock – with the added bonus of enough meat after cooking to make a second dish.

CINNAMON STICKS boiled in water on the stove make a lovely house fragrance.

CITRUS fruit releases more juice if the fruit is warmed in a bowl of hot water before juicing.

CITRUS zest is easier to grate if you wet the grater first.

DRIED FRUIT will not stick to the blade if chopped with a wet knife.

EGGS can be tested before cooking by popping into a bowl of salted water. Good eggs sink. Bad eggs bob to the top.

EGG WHITES will keep for several days in the fridge in a tightly-sealed container. EGG YOLKS can also be saved like this if they are first covered with water.

HERB VINEGAR, about two teaspoonsful, added to the water for poaching eggs, gives a pleasant extra flavour and helps to prevent sticking.

ICE CUBES dropped into soups or stews are a quick way of reducing fat. The fat will congeal around the ice.

KIWI FRUIT is full of good human nutrition – vitamin C, potassium, vitamin E, folic acid and fibre. It also contains an enzyme called actinidin, which is an excellent meat tenderiser.

Place slices of kiwi fruit on the meat or spread it pureed on meat which has been forked to allow impregnation. For finely sliced stir-fry steaks, a few minutes is sufficient. The rule is 30 minutes per 2.5 centimetre thickness of meat. Meat can then be wiped and grilled, or, if being casseroled, cooked with the marinade still on it.

WARNING: This is not an overnight treatment. If you leave your meat soaking in kiwi fruit, it may turn to mush.

LEFTOVER JAMS AND JELLIES can be mixed and stored in one jar to be used as glazes on hams or roasts.

LEFTOVER TEA OR COFFEE can be recycled by freezing in cube trays, then popping it into freezer bags and later using in iced tea or coffee drinks. This provides ice that does not water down the drink.

LEMONS can be pierced with a skewer and squeezed, then wrapped in clingfilm for further use when recipes only call for one teaspoon of juice.

MILK used for soaking or poaching will reduce the flavour of strong-flavoured fish, or a dash added to water when cooking cauliflower will help to keep it white.

MUSTARD POWDER in the washing up water helps to kill fish smells on implements.

NUTMEG is supposed to be good for lessening the after-perfuming of garlic on the breath. Finely-grated nutmeg mixed with salt and made into a paste with crushed garlic is a tasty addition to mashed potatoes.

OATBRAN is good for lowering cholesterol and a great substitute for bread-crumbs (fish fillets dusted in oatmeal and seasoning are brilliant) as well as an effective thickening agent in soups and even bol sauce – and quite pleasant added to scrambled egg.

OATMEAL is a life-giving healthfood and a superior thickener. Instant porridge is a smart anti-cholesterol way to thicken strongly-flavoured soups or even bolognaise sauces.

OIL – just a few drops – will stop pasta water from boiling over.

ONIONS AND POTATOES should not be stored together. Potatoes rot quickly when near onions. Instead, store potatoes in a plastic bag along with an apple. This will help stop them from sprouting.

ORANGE AND LEMON RINDS need not be wasted just because the juice is needed. Grated, they freeze well and make a lovely addition to cakes and stews. Orange peel goes well in beef stews and lemon with veal or chicken.

ORANGE JUICE is better than water as an addition to omelettes to make them lighter.

PASSIONFRUIT transforms any fruit salad into a sensational dessert.

PLASTIC FOOD-STORAGE CONTAINERS can be placed in the sunshine to help rid them of food stains.

PARSLEY freezes well in plastic bags and does not have to be defrosted for use – just clip with scissors from the frozen bunch and return it to the freezer. CHIVES and other HERBS can be treated similarly.

ROSEMARY by the branch or mass of sprigs, placed on a baking tray in a warm oven, emits delightful aromas which make for one of the nicest house-deodorisers in the business.

SALAD OIL splashed on the clothes can be stopped in its spread by the immediate application of talcum powder – and removed altogether by a soak in a borax/water mix.

SALTY SOUP can be salvaged by peeling and slicing a potato and cooking it in the soup, and removing it before serving.

SAMBAL is the Indonesian name given to chili paste. There are as many sorts of chili paste as there are moods in a teenager. Sambal Oelek is probably the most useful variety to have in the kitchen and to place on the table as a condiment. There are dark sambals and light sambals, each with their own flavours and culinary purpose. You can buy good sambals at any supermarket, and specialist varieties in Chinese supermarkets. Crushed chili paste is a reasonable substitute, as are some of the chili sauces on the supermarket shelves.

You can always add chili to a meal but you can't take it out. Thus is it advisable to go carefully in preparation and offer the option of extra on the table. One of my favourite ways of doing this is to chop some fresh, tiny hot chilies and mix them into a small bowl of light soy sauce. This is superb on rice or with any Asian-style meal.

SCISSORS! You can't have too many pairs of scissors in the kitchen. They are useful for snipping chives and herbs and chopping salad. They are brilliant for cutting the crusts off bread and even cutting toast into fingers. There is almost no limit to their handiness.

STALE CAKE can have its moisture replenished by placing it in a colander over boiling water until it becomes soft to touch.

TWEEZERS are great for pulling bones from fish.

UNSALTED BUTTER works better for greasing baking pans than salted butter.

VINEGAR is my mother's favourite household helper. She bulk buys cheap supermarket vinegar. Some of its uses:
- mixed fifty–fifty with hot water it gives a final rinse to make anything glass sparkle when air-dried
- a scant cup in the washing machine rinse cycle whitens and brightens
- two tablespoons in a bucket of water make a good window-cleaner (decant it into a spray container for ease)
- if one is plagued by an excess of suds bubbling back up in a sink, a splash of vinegar in the second rinse will fix things
- rubbed on the hands, it will remove odours after handling fish
- poured into a bowl and placed on a window it will freshen the air of cigarette or stale smells.

Index of Recipes

Wakefield Press is an independent publishing and
distribution company based in Adelaide, South Australia.
We love good stories and publish beautiful books.
To see our full range of titles, please visit our website at
www.wakefieldpress.com.au.